THE
MAKING
OF
BILLY
BISHOP

THE MAKING OF BILLY BISHOP

The First World War Exploits of Billy Bishop, VC

Brereton Greenhous

THE DUNDURN GROUP
TORONTO · OXFORD

Copy-editor: Lloyd Davis
Designer: Jennifer Scott
Printer:Transcontinental

National Library of Canada Cataloguing in Publication Data

Greenhous, Brereton, 1929–
The making of Billy Bishop

Includes bibliographical references and index.
ISBN 1-55002-390-X

1. Bishop, William A., 1894–1956. 2. World War, 1914–1918 — Aerial operations, British. 3. Great Britain. Royal Flying Corps — Biography. 4. Fighter pilots — Canada — Biography. I. Title.

D602.G74 2002   940.4'4971'092   C2002-901064-0

1   2   3   4   5   06   05   04   03   02

We acknowledge the support of the **Canada Council for the Arts** and the **Ontario Arts Council** for our publishing program. We also acknowledge the financial support of the **Government of Canada** through the **Book Publishing Industry Development Program** and **The Association for the Export of Canadian Books**, and the **Government of Ontario** through the **Ontario Book Publishers Tax Credit** program.

Care has been taken to trace the ownership of copyright material used in this book. The author and the publisher welcome any information enabling them to rectify any references or credit in subsequent editions.

J. Kirk Howard, President

Printed and bound in Canada.⊗
Printed on recycled paper.
www.dundurn.com

Dundurn Press	Dundurn Press	Dundurn Press
8 Market Street	73 Lime Walk	2250 Military Road
Suite 200	Headington, Oxford,	Tonawanda NY
Toronto, Ontario, Canada	England	U.S.A. 14150
M5E 1M6	OX3 7AD	

In Memory Of
Lieutenant
ERNEST BRERETON GREENHOUS
1st Battalion, Royal Scots Fusiliers
and
Number 9 Squadron, Royal Flying Corps

Killed in action
in the air over Flanders
26 August 1917

TABLE OF CONTENTS

ACKNOWLEDGMENTS   9
INTRODUCTION   11

CHAPTER 1: "The Greatest Game in the World"   29
CHAPTER 2: A Pilot at the Front   55
CHAPTER 3: Tricks of the Trade   81
CHAPTER 4: Flight of Fancy   107
CHAPTER 5: Flying High   129
CHAPTER 6: A Statistical Interlude   151
CHAPTER 7: "I Have Never Been So Furious in My Life"   169

EPILOGUE   199
APPENDIX   207
ENDNOTES   211
PUBLISHER'S AFTERWORD   225
INDEX   227

MAPS: Bishop's Bases and Units in France, 1917–1918   54
      Possible Bishop Targets, 2 June 1917   106

Show me a hero and I will write you a tragedy.
— F. Scott Fitzgerald, *Notebooks* [1978]

ACKNOWLEDGMENTS

M y debt to the late Phil Markham goes beyond words. He was a knowledgeable researcher and a regrettably modest gentleman. I say "regrettably" because that modesty made him reluctant to place his meticulous explorations of the Bishop canon before the public. I (and others) spent several years, on and off, trying to persuade him to put his evidence and conclusions into print, and happily, shortly before his death, he did publish his paper on "The Early Hours of 2 June 1917" in a specialist American journal. I have reached different conclusions about Bishop's possible destinations that day, but we shared a common disbelief in Bishop's account of where he went and what happened, and my explication owes much to Phil's original research. His widow, Jo, was good enough to give me access to his papers.

Arthur Bishop did scholarship a service when he deposited originals and/or copies of his father's papers with the Department of National Defence's Directorate of History (as it was then known), making them available without restriction to interested historians. I have mixed feelings about using them to question and partially destroy the reputation of their originator, but I am truly grateful for the access thus provided.

My sister, Anne Thomas, was good enough to investigate many British sources on my behalf and provided invaluable assistance before her sudden and unexpected death in February 2000. For these and many other kindnesses, I remember her with great affection. I am also grateful to the following (in alphabetical order) for their support, advice and/or assistance: Yilmas Alimoglu, Serge Bernier, John Bruce, David Campbell, Isabel Campbell, Tim Dubé, Norman Franks, Bill Glover, Hugh Halliday, Steve Harris, Sean and Andrew Horrall, Chris Johnson (who drew the maps), Madeleine Lafleur-Lemire, Gerry LaForce, Paul Lansey, David and Michael McNorgan, Ed Patten, Ken Reynolds, Lloyd Strickland and Mike Whitby.

Nevertheless, the conception and interpretation of Bishop's exploits presented here is essentially my own. So are any errors that may have crept in. Mine, all mine! But I hope to God none have, for diehard worshippers of the Bishop canon (and there are certainly many of them) will no doubt be searching for a metaphorical stick with which to beat me.

INTRODUCTION

Now for the purpose of attaining an end so desirable
as that of rewarding individual instances of merit
and valour We have instituted and created ... a new
Naval and Military Decoration which We are
desirous should be highly prized and eagerly sought
after by the Officers and Men of Our Naval and
Military Services.

The Victoria Cross, the British Commonwealth's greatest
acknowledgment of physical courage, was created in 1856 to
recognize outstanding feats of bravery in the Crimean War
(1854–1856) and in future conflicts. Over the years, the ratio
between those eligible to receive the Cross and those upon whom it
has actually been bestowed has made it the rarest of all decorations
awarded for acts of valour — rarer than the United States' Medal of
Honor; rarer than Imperial Germany's *Pour le Mérite*, the Third
Reich's *Ritterkreuz*, with its various trimmings of oak leaves, swords
and diamonds, or the former Soviet Union's *Geroj SSSR Medalj*

Zolotaja Zvezda; rarer, even, than the now-forgotten Austrian and Russian Orders of Maria Theresa and St. George, upon which the VC concept appears to have been based.[1]

Nevertheless, some earlier awards were made on rather generous grounds in light of the First World War (1914–1918), a doleful but numinous experience that raised the bar considerably. In 1918, Rear Admiral Sir A.F. Everett, the naval representative on a committee considering the revision of the appropriate Royal Warrant, noted that "the standard of valour and devotion to duty for the Victoria Cross is now very much higher than it was in the earlier years of its introduction."[2] An exception, perhaps, was the case of Second Lieutenant W. Leefe Robinson, who won his in September 1916 for shooting down, with the new incendiary ammunition, the first Zeppelin to be destroyed over England, even though the only significant risk he ran was the (not inconsiderable) one inherent in night flying at that time. Robinson's was surely a politically motivated award if ever there was one, handed down by an intensely relieved bureaucracy fearful of a restive population suddenly and painfully exposed to the horrors of aerial bombardment.

The original Warrant stipulated that the senior officer of the unit or formation concerned, upon initiating a VC recommendation, "shall call for such description and attestation of the act as he may think requisite" before forwarding it to the War Office or Admiralty. During the South African War (1899–1902) this became, in practice, a requirement for at least two eyewitnesses. They might be totally illiterate, as in the case of Sergeant N.G. Leakey, King's African Rifles, who won his posthumous VC in Abyssinia in 1941, his valour attested to by witnesses who signed their statements with thumbprints. They might even be found among the ranks of the enemy, as with Flying Officer L.A. Trigg, DFC, of the Royal New Zealand Air Force, whose aircraft was shot down with the loss of all on board when attacking a surfaced submarine off the West African coast in 1943. It was left to survivors of the sunken U-boat to confirm the courage and determination with which Trigg had pressed home his attack.

But one way or another, there were almost always witnesses. Only two VCs have ever been awarded without any. One was granted (very reluctantly, in return for a Medal of Honor already presented by Act of Congress to the Empire's Unknown Soldier) to the American Unknown Warrior of World War I.[3] The other went to Captain William Avery "Billy" Bishop, a Canadian from Owen Sound, Ontario, then serving in the Royal Flying Corps, for an attack on a German airfield allegedly carried out on 2 June 1917.

Bishop had already been officially credited with twenty-two aerial victories when he won his VC, and he would add another fifty to his total before his combat career came to an end on 19 June 1918. A darling of his RFC superiors, as well as British and Canadian society and the international media, his spectacular record caused him to be placed ninth in a popular ranking of Canada's greatest heroes as reported by the *National Post*[4] — more than eighty years after his fighting career ended and forty-three years after his death.

But I contend that the attack that brought Bishop his VC never happened, and that many of those seventy-two victories were the product of an ambitious imagination that was encouraged by the authorities. Billy Bishop was a brave flyer — and a consummate, bold liar.

His courage was never in doubt. When Bishop first left the ground (as an observer, in the fall of 1915), aircraft were still apt to crash at any moment due to engine or structural failure. Flying skills were similarly undeveloped. No one fully understood the principles of flight, which made flying a very dangerous occupation, with one accidental death for every ninety hours of flying training[5] and an indeterminate number of serious injuries in the same time span. (One such crippled pilot was destined to play a major role in furthering Bishop's career.) And when an airman reached the front, where hostile guns — in the air and on the ground — were added to the inherent dangers of flight, only the luckiest and most skilful survived for more than a few weeks.

A bullet through a vital organ was the kindest way to die. Aircraft constructed of wire, wood and fabric, powered by gasoline-fuelled engines in an age before self-sealing tanks, easily became "flamers" as bullets reached their target, leaving the unfortunate occupants a choice between burning to death or jumping to their doom. Parachutes existed, and were issued to balloon observers, but there were none for the members of the Royal Flying Corps (RFC) or the Royal Naval Air Service (RNAS). Seat packs had not yet been devised, existing 'chutes were bulky, heavy and awkward to manipulate in cramped cockpits, and there was a general accept-ance by flying men that they were impractical. In 1918, the German air service did begin to issue parachutes to all its airmen, but the Royal Air Force (and Royal Canadian Air Force) did not do so until 1924.

Under such circumstances, to fly at all required considerable courage; to fly into battle, even more. Few men could withstand the anxieties of combat flying for very long, and many a potential ace could not bring himself to fly again after escaping a crash with even minor injuries. Lester Pearson, who would one day become the four-teenth prime minister of Canada — and eventually be ranked above Bishop in the *National Post's* pantheon of popular heroes — joined the Royal Flying Corps in October 1917. When he began pilot train-ing he looked forward, in his own words, to becoming "Sir Lester, knight of the azure blue," but that was not to be. He was still under instruction when the engine of his machine failed at a height of some seven hundred feet. His instructor brought the aircraft down to a crash landing in which neither pilot nor pupil was seriously injured, both escaping with "a good shaking up and some cuts." That experience, not uncommon for the time, brought an end to Pearson's dream. He made one more flight, but in August 1918 he was invalided out of the service suffering from "neurasthenia — a generalized anxiety syndrome."[6] Put simply, when it came to flying, he had lost his nerve, like many a good man before and after him.

Bishop, on the other hand, survived many minor crashes, both in training and in France, and was engaged in an uncertain but considerable number of potentially fatal combats at a time when British airmen were falling like flies to German guns. He never lost his nerve — although, as we shall see, once or twice he perhaps came close! Like every other sane airman, he felt the strain and paid a psychological price. No one in his right mind was fully immune to the stresses of flying and combat.

Regrettably, human psyches seem to need heroic models, to such an extent that, if they do not exist, we must create them. For the lucky few, wars provide serendipitous occasions to achieve such distinction, and Bishop was not slow to take advantage of his good luck or his subsequent celebrity when the opportunity arose. While on leave in Canada during the winter of 1917–18, shortly after adding the VC to his first Distinguished Service Order and his Military Cross, he put his name to a memoir of his military service to date, entitled *Winged Warfare*.

Since, at the same time, he was busy (a) getting married and honeymooning, and (b) crisscrossing North America making patriotic speeches and hobnobbing with the high and the mighty, how did he find the time to write a book between mid-September 1917 and the end of January 1918? For a foundation, he had his logbook, possibly copies of his combat reports, and the many letters that he had mailed home to fiancée and family. Both his letters and his combat reports show a simple, unsophisticated facility with words appropriate to a bright young middle-class male. There is no evidence that a ghost writer was employed. The texts of later editions were expanded and polished, but I have chosen to use only the 1918 edition — completed within nine months of the events it describes — and have treated it as a primary document, more or less on a par with his letters and combat reports, in the chapters that follow. The book was a bestseller, just as his fellow Canadian and fervent admirer, Lord Beaverbrook, had assured him it would be. Royalties might add up to "[t]housands of dollars, even pounds," Bishop noted, hopefully.[7] And so they did.

Thirteen years after *Winged Warfare* was published, George Drew — then a Guelph lawyer and businessman and subsequently to become premier of Ontario — penned *Canada's Fighting Airmen*, an ingratiating account of the feats of the country's leading air aces, in which Bishop automatically took pride of place. Drew did not do any original research into his subjects' combat records, however, and his version of Bishop is simply a sycophantic rewrite of *Winged Warfare*.

Through the later 1930s, the Second World War, and the postwar decades, a number of articles in Canadian, British and American newspapers and popular magazines have recounted Bishop's alleged accomplishments — most of them written by journalistic drudges, a few by old comrades-in-arms happy to turn a doubtful dollar by jumping on the Bishop bandwagon. They embellished the legend buttressed by *Canada's Fighting Airmen*, sometimes to the point of absurdity, and today they are all best ignored and forgotten.

In the years following Billy Bishop's death, Arthur Bishop, himself a Second World War pilot in the RCAF (between them, father and son were credited with destroying seventy-three enemy aircraft!) wrote *The Courage of the Early Morning: A Son's Biography of his Famous*

Father. Admitting to indulging in "poetic licence,"[8] Arthur carried the story on through the Second World War — when his father's "cold blue reviewing eye"[9] and his multifarious rows of medals (one of which, as we shall see, he was certainly not entitled to wear) were an inspiration to thousands of young pilots graduating from the British Commonwealth Air Training Plan — all the way to his peaceful passing at Palm Beach, Florida, in September 1956. Perhaps the best, and surely the truest, thing about Arthur's book was the title, taken from a dictum of Napoleon's that the courage of the early morning was the rarest kind of courage.

Another fourteen years passed, and the legend finally began to crumble. At first it just bowed slightly when, in 1969, the Vancouver East Cultural Centre staged an offbeat kind of play — one actor playing many parts, accompanied on a piano by the playwright — under the rubric *Billy Bishop Goes to War.* (The production subsequently moved to Ottawa, and then to New York.) John Gray's script essentially followed the legend as laid down in *Winged Warfare* and *The Courage of the Early Morning*, but Eric Peterson, who played the parts of Bishop and everyone else, spent some time at the Department of National Defence's Directorate of History, going through the files on Bishop and getting a feel for the man that went beyond the words in the script. After poring over copies of Bishop's correspondence, he accurately portrayed a man who was egotistical, inhumanly ambitious, and not really very likeable at all.

"Here was this guy talking in almost schoolboy terms," said Peterson, "about the destruction of other human beings without an emotional qualm." Meanwhile, John Gray explained that "the [chauvinistic] ending of the play is meant to be ironic in the extreme." Nevertheless, because the script never actually questioned Bishop's record, the play aroused no vehement opposition. Indeed, it was widely praised by critics and audiences, many of whom interpreted the finale as "a thumping call to arms."[10]

It was left to a National Film Board producer, Paul Cowan, to raise some truly iconoclastic questions in his 1982 documentary, *The Kid Who Couldn't Miss*. While he never explicitly said so, Cowan managed to suggest that much of Bishop's combat record was faked. In particular, he questioned the validity of the alleged raid in the early morning hours of 2 June 1917 that brought Bishop his Victoria Cross. From Newfoundland to Vancouver Island, middle-aged and elderly Canadians (mostly veterans — young people didn't seem to care so much) rose up in patriotic wrath. How dare some jumped-up young filmmaker attack a national icon! And they had plenty of material to work with in Cowan's abuse of historical sequence and use of fictitious personalities and dialogue whenever the real things were unavailable. Whatever its artistic merits, as history the film is a sloppy, vulgar piece of work which nevertheless raises a valid issue: was Bishop a liar and a fraud?

A national hero mangled but hardly cleansed in the washtub of dramatized history, and at public expense, to boot! The Senate of Canada got involved, and its subcommittee on veterans' affairs was charged with examining the accuracy and propriety of the film. Since the subcommittee was composed largely of veterans of the Second World War brought up on the Bishop legend (and since one and all, as senators, had a vested interest in preserving the status quo), the result was easily foreseeable.

Canadian historians of repute were asked to express their opinions, and the best of them cheerily talked his way around the core issue. The subcommittee judged it unnecessary to bring potentially hostile witnesses from Britain and the United States, but called upon a plethora of sympathetic locals. There was much ad hominem argument; several enraged senators and a number of indignant, self-styled "experts" enthusiastically defended Bishop on the simple — and simplistic — grounds that he was a great man, a great Canadian, and therefore not to be attacked or criticized by lesser men. They found nothing good to say about Cowan's work — and much to criticize — but neither could they produce any primary evidence to authenticate their hero's VC exploit.

Finally, a hard-pressed NFB agreed to label the film as "docudrama," which is undoubtedly what it was, but Bishop's more ardent supporters were not so easily assuaged. One of them, Cliff Chadderton, the chief executive officer of the War Amputations of Canada and a long-time, powerful advocate of veterans' causes, prepared and published a vacuous 370-page digest of the controversy. *Hanging a Legend: The National Film Board's Shameful Attempt to Discredit Billy Bishop, VC* purported to "consolidate between two covers all of the relevant material pertaining to this issue." Describing Cowan's work as "an insulting and disgraceful profile of a national war hero," Chadderton defended Bishop's record largely on the basis that "it has been universally accepted by all established military historians.[11]

He had a genuine point there, one which deserves some consideration. "All" is an all-encompassing word, but I for one do not know of any professional historian who had questioned the Bishop legend before Cowan did so. Only a few dedicated amateurs, such as Phil Markham in Canada and Ed Ferko in the United States, were privately doubting his claims. However, in the Notes and Comments section of the June 1989 issue of the *Canadian Historical Review*, I made an initial attempt to revise the professional view in an item entitled "The Sad Case of Billy Bishop, VC." It aroused singularly little interest — nothing like the furore that had followed my Bishop entry in the second edition of *The Canadian Encyclopaedia*, in which I had innocently (and truthfully) remarked of the Senate enquiry that "the senators were unable to demonstrate that Bishop's claims were valid." That prompted a number of demands — some from quite prominent citizens — that I be fired from my job at the Department of National Defence. It also garnered a threat on my life from a gentleman in Cape Breton, whose quavering handwriting suggested that he was either too old to carry out his vendetta, or quite breathless with anticipation.

As for Bishop's seventy-two alleged victories, even professional historians have long accepted that the claims of many First World War British fighter pilots were grossly exaggerated. German claims were generally valid, since the vast majority of air fighting took place over or behind their lines and the physical remnants of fallen aircraft could usually be located and assigned to specific claimants. With Teutonic thoroughness, German authorities insisted that claims be correlated with crashes. The RFC/RAF, on the other hand, had to rely largely on reports from the airmen concerned, and as the war progressed squadron commanders became less and less particular about corroboration; as casualties mounted, higher authorities, too, became more lax in their acceptance of claims.

The matter was complicated by the changing nature of air fighting.

> The exaggerated claims of 1917 and 1918 were brought about not by deliberate misrepresentation but by the ever more rigorous exigencies of combat flying. Early in the war, when the air environment was one of relatively low intensity, when aircraft were slower and less manoeuvrable, tactics rudimentary, and the cubic area of combat significantly less due to

operational ceilings, claims were likely to be much more reliable. At that time a victorious pilot could often afford to follow a solitary enemy down, to deliver another burst or two of fire to make sure of his victim and to report the co-ordinates of the point at which he saw the enemy crash. By 1918 fighters had an operational ceiling of at least three-and-a-half miles, speeds of well over 160 mph could be reached in a dive, airframes were stronger, firepower was more than doubled, and a cubic mile of airspace might contain a hundred weaving, diving, circling aircraft between two cloud layers. The pilot who kept his eyes fixed on a single enemy machine for more than a few seconds was likely to be shot down himself.[12]

Increasingly, credit was granted to a claimant — especially one with an established reputation — without any supporting evidence. Moreover, only the British recognized the "driven down out of control" (DDOOC) category as a victory,[13] so that the claims of British pilots — *all* British pilots, not only Bishop — were coloured by considerable hyperbole. "In the later stages of the war, it is also necessary to observe both sides exploited the propaganda value of successes in the air battle. It was probably not entirely coincidental that air staffs gradually relaxed the criteria they employed to determine when a combat victory had been won."[14]

The best examples of British insouciance in this regard come from the late spring and summer of 1918, including the four unbelievable weeks during which Bishop would increase his tally sufficiently to make him the top-scoring British ace.* In May 1918, the Royal Air

---

* In the post-war era Major Edward Mannock's acolyte, Ira Jones, would bloat his idol's total to 73! Mannock's posthumous VC citation gave his total as fifty.

Force (as it had become on 1 April) asserted that it had destroyed 378 enemy machines, with another 95 driven down out of control, while losing 126 of its own. Actual German losses were 150. In June, the RAF laid claim to another 340 victims, while the Germans only lost 150. These kinds of statistics expose to ridicule the records of men like Bishop, or his fellow Canadian Donald MacLaren, who was credited with his first victim on 6 March 1918 and his fifty-fourth (!) on 9 October 1918.[16]

Bishop's next biographer of note, Dan McCaffery, a newspaper-man from Sarnia, Ontario, corresponded with several of Bishop's former comrades (a privilege that the passing years have denied me) in researching *Billy Bishop: Canadian Hero*, stretching to find eyewitnesses to his hero's claims but not pursuing doubts or discrepancies to their logical conclusions. "It was not uncommon in aerial combat for a man to submit accurate reports until he built up an impressive score and then, with an inflated opinion of his own ability, to begin over-claiming," McCaffery admits. But Bishop, he asserts, was not such a man, although "it is possible that, on a few isolated occasions, he was overly optimistic in his claims."[17] McCaffery goes on to concede that "it would seem that about two dozen of Billy's victories, although claimed in good faith as down out of control, driven down or forced to land, should be subtracted from his total because they were not true 'kills.'"[18]

When it came to consideration of the alleged raid on a German airfield that brought Bishop his Victoria Cross, however, McCaffery found nothing strange about Bishop's account. He was happy to take a number of very doubtful supplementary sources at their word, no matter how bizarre their stories, and to incorporate much of his own vivid imagination in confirming Bishop's claim. At the same time, he recorded honestly that in 1977 three out of four of Bishop's surviving comrades from 60 Squadron days had declined to sign an RAF Museum first-day cover bearing a stamp commemorating the VC raid.[19]

Why, you may ask, did these doubting Thomases not raise their misgivings at the time? Well, such serious allegations were not made easily when there was no prima facie way to refute Bishop's claim. There was no question that the man was extraordinarily brave in an environment in which courage counted for much. Then again, as we shall see, their commanding officer in 60 Squadron, Major A.J.L. Scott, much their senior in years and worldly experience as well as in rank, had initially encouraged Bishop to exaggerate his claims and apparently had no qualms about believing his protégé's account of his early-morning flight; Scott went as far as to report the tale to his superiors within hours — perhaps even minutes — of Bishop's return. That would have given skeptics little time to consider and express any doubts before the matter reached higher authorities, who were just as willing as Scott to believe Bishop's yarn.

To have publicly questioned their comrade's credibility after that would have exposed Scott, a man whom they greatly respected for reasons that will become obvious, to severe criticism, and would have brought down upon their heads the wrath of more senior officers desperately trying to create an RFC hero to compete against the great "Red Baron," Manfred von Richthofen. Nor could they have dreamt that Bishop was going to get a VC out of it until the deed was done. Half a century of reflection, and the knowledge that all the major figures involved were long dead, probably cast a very different light on things.

The next contribution of interest came from William D. Mathieson, a high school history teacher, who produced a slim (63-page) soft-cover volume, entitled simply *Billy Bishop, VC*. His acknowledgments make it clear that this work owed much to Bishop's daughter and granddaughter, and his conclusions are therefore those that might be expected. The work is of interest chiefly because it includes quotations from Bishop's correspondence with his family in 1914–15 — letters that are not included among those held at the Department of National Defence's Directorate of History and Heritage.

The most recent work on Bishop is a chapter in David L. Bashow's *Knights of the Air: Canadian Fighter Pilots in the First World War*, a kind of superior successor to George Drew's book. Bashow is, or was, an RCAF pilot who relies heavily on too many sources of the Chadderton and McCaffrey sort, as well as the work of Bishop aficionado Stewart Taylor. Consequently, he has no difficulty in accepting the traditional view of an "incomparable" Billy Bishop.

If Cowan had raised some iconoclastic questions, Timothy Graves and the late Philip Markham provided some equally intriguing answers in two post-Cowan articles. In the late 1980s, Graves, a British researcher,* set himself the somewhat daunting task of going through the combat reports of the five leading British aces, one by one, and assessing the validity of their claims against a common standard. He then argued that just five of the forty-seven victories attributed to Bishop while he was with 60 Squadron were independently witnessed. (I can only find three, perhaps four — see Chapter 6.) Another eighteen, he thought, were probably valid, even though they were unconfirmed, for a total of twenty-three. "This reassessment is not a flippant or ill-conceived attempt to discredit Bishop," wrote Charles Messenger, the editor of *World War II Investigator*,** in an accompanying commentary, "but rather a means of redressing

---

* Graves served a prison sentence for stealing military records from the Public Record Office in London, but that does not invalidate his research. Indeed, it might be interpreted as strengthening it.

** On this special occasion, despite the title, investigating an aspect of World War I.

the balance of objectivity by treating each pilot's victory claims in an identical fashion."[20]

If Bishop's victories while with 60 Squadron were about half the total of his claims, as Graves suggests, then he was approximating the average for British pilots in the last two years of the war in light of British claims and actual German losses. But when he was his own commanding officer with 85 Squadron in the early summer of 1918, and thus his own confirming authority, the proportion of arguably false claims would rise substantially. By my count, his final tally of witnessed victories was *four* out of the seventy-two he was credited with! Perhaps another twenty or so were genuine but uncorroborated — still a more-than-respectable score. Most of the remainder were deliberate misrepresentations on his part — many of them fostered, if not actually abetted, by his superiors.

Returning in 1995 to the raid that brought Bishop his VC, Philip Markham, an aero-engineer and former pilot himself, published an article in *Over the Front* — the journal of the League of World War I Aviation Historians — that incorporated twenty-five years of meticulous research. He concluded:

> My attempt to confirm Bishop's claim to have attacked an enemy aerodrome and to have destroyed three enemy aircraft on 2 June 1917 has been altogether unsuccessful. I have been unable to discover any supporting evidence; in fact it has been quite the reverse.
>
> The point has come when the facts must be faced, when the opinion of his comrades and contemporaries that Bishop was a fake … must be taken seriously, and weighed against the character of the man.[21]

The chapter of this book that examines the circumstances of Bishop's alleged raid relies heavily upon Phil Markham's research, and the rest of the work is an attempt to illustrate "the character of the man" by his day-to-day actions, as Phil believed should be done to make the case against him complete.

At first sight it seems odd that M.J. Crook's absorbing work *The Evolution of the Victoria Cross: A Study in Administrative History* does not deal with Bishop's VC in the chapter devoted to "difficult cases." However, in another context, Crook refers to "the almost complete destruction of the W[ar] O[ffice] files relating to the award of the VC during the Great War,"[22] which goes far toward explaining why no one has been able to find the paperwork surrounding Bishop's award and why he did not touch the Bishop case.

Should the documentation be uncovered by some miracle, what might it prove? It still would not — indeed, *could* not — show through a series of cold, hard facts that the raid took place. There was never any evidence of it from the German side, then or later, and we have only Bishop's unsubstantiated word on the British side. However, the missing paperwork might clarify the reasoning that led the authorities to grant the award despite a lack of witnesses. It might, for example, demonstrate that the British "establishment," both civil and military, was anxious to create an air hero to rival or match Germany's Red Baron in a war in which propaganda was playing an ever-increasing part.

Despite the increasing, and increasingly obvious, importance of public relations, Whitehall resolutely refused to advertise the feats of individual airmen, even while British newspapers were quoting French and German communiqués that specifically named their aces. Thus *The Times* of 3 May 1917 mentioned two German aces by name in recounting their growing number of victories, while British aces had only ever been mentioned by name when they won VCs. And there was little enough occasion to mention any of them in the spring and summer of 1917: Lanoe Hawker and Albert Ball (whose Cross was awarded posthumously), were both dead by the summer of 1917; Lionel Rees, no longer fit for operational flying, was commanding a flying school back in England; and Leefe Robinson, while leading a flight of two-seater Bristol Fighters from 48 Squadron, had fallen into enemy hands on 5 April 1917 and would spend the remainder of the war in a German prison camp.[23] They could no longer fuel an embryonic propaganda machine; but Billy Bishop, on the other hand, was a living, breathing, operationally active ace — and good-looking and charming, to boot!

Perhaps the uncorroborated acceptance of Bishop's VC story was also connected to the War Office's anxiety to pay tribute to the substantial and ever-growing Canadian part in the air war, in an effort to divert growing pressure for an independent Canadian air force. By the summer of 1917, a quarter of the aircrew in the British flying services were Canadian, and their transfer to a Canadian air arm would have crippled both the RFC and the RNAS.[24] Again, a paper trail might illustrate the strength of Bishop's social connections, developed while he was on leave in England and which, as we shall see, even reached into the royal family. On the other hand, Whitehall could hardly reveal that his story was no more than a piece of extempore invention designed simply to enhance his growing reputation and to further his private agenda of becoming the top-scoring fighter pilot of the war. Had that become common knowledge, there would have been no VC. Some other likely lad would have had to be groomed for glory.

It is, of course, impossible to prove negatives with hard data. Those who dispute the case against Bishop can always argue that there must be other unrevealed or unrecorded facts that would confirm his assertions. This is especially true of the claim that brought Bishop his Victoria Cross, the one decoration above all others that has always been seen as absolutely immaculate — beyond any reproach or criticism — because of the rules surrounding its award. How, then, can the unbeliever make his case?

To put the matter in quasi-legal terms, a prosecutor endeavouring to prove Bishop a liar and a fraud must rely on circumstantial proofs. Moreover, since there is likely to be some testimony, however slight, available to the defence, he must provide an overwhelming weight of contrary evidence if he is to win a conviction. Sticking with the legal analogy, the accused may be found guilty "beyond a reasonable doubt," or, if that standard will not hold, on a balance of probabilities, as in a civil trial. If the verdict in either case is "guilty," are there extenuating circumstances? If so, what are they? Or, of course, the accused may be acquitted of all charges. Eighty-odd years after the fact, whatever it may be, the reader must reach his own verdict and decide upon the appropriate penalty.

CHAPTER 1

"The Greatest Game in the World"

William Avery Bishop was born, fair-haired and blue-eyed, on 9 February 1894, at Owen Sound, Ontario, the third and youngest son of Will and Margaret Bishop. Will was an undistinguished lawyer by trade, a Liberal by choice, and registrar of Grey County by vocation. His eldest son, Worth, was ten years older than Billy. A second son, Kilbourne, had been born two years after Worth, but died in 1903 at the age of seven. A sister, Louise, completed the family in 1895.

Judging from his appearance in later years, Billy must have been a handsome lad of compact, medium proportions. He spoke with a nascent lisp. Psychologically, he was something of a nonconformist by the standards of rural Ontario at the turn of the century. He was never keen on the usual team sports that engrossed most adolescent boys — baseball, lacrosse, hockey — preferring such individual diversions as swimming, riding (he had his own horse) and rough shooting. His riding and shooting skills were to serve him well in the years to come. More unusually, he was apparently the only young male in Owen Sound who obviously enjoyed attending dancing classes,[1] although there was nothing effeminate about him.

In 1910, when he was sixteen, he met a visitor from Toronto: Margaret Burden, granddaughter of the millionaire Timothy Eaton of department store fame. While Billy apparently flirted enthusiastically with any number of other girls, then and later, he took Margaret rather more seriously. Late in 1917, after winning his Victoria Cross, he would marry her. Meanwhile, it was mightily important to him that he find whatever ways he could of dazzling her and, perhaps more crucially, given the mores of the time, impressing her parents. To just what extent that impulse drove him in his wartime quest for glory we can only speculate, but it may well have been a significant element.

For the moment, it was hard to see how he could impress anyone. His lowly academic stature, due perhaps more to a lack of interest than of intellect, made university an unlikely proposition, for at that time Canada's few universities were very much realms of academic excellence. However, the Royal Military College of Canada, at Kingston, Ontario — from which his brother Worth had graduated in 1903, tenth out of twenty-six* — had lower academic standards then than it does today. Upon graduation it offered a diploma rather than a degree and a commission in the militia. Normally, only the top two or three graduates would be offered commissions in either the British Army or Canada's minuscule Permanent Force. RMC's emphasis on engineering, combined with Will Bishop's Liberal party connections, raised the possibility of Billy following Worth into the ranks of the federal

---

* Arthur Bishop, in his father's biography, *The Courage of the Early Morning*, wrongly states that Worth graduated "with the highest standard ever attained by a cadet." I am indebted for his true ranking, and most of the material in this chapter relating to Billy's time at RMC, to an unpublished research paper by (then) Gentleman Cadet J.R. McKenzie, "The Real Case of No. 943 William Avery Bishop." (Copy in DHH, Bishop biog. file.)

Department of Public Works — not a particularly auspicious appointment, but one that would offer security and a certain minimal status in society.

Billy "crammed" for an entrance examination in which he placed forty-second out of the forty-three who passed, but his marginal entrance marks gave an accurate indication of what was to come. In a vain endeavour to scrape through his first-year examination, he was caught cheating in some unspecified manner and "rusticated," or temporarily suspended. College regulations stipulated that:

> If a Cadet affords to, or obtains from another Cadet, any assistance during an examination, or if he makes use of any improper means of obtaining information relative to an examination he will, if it be his final examination for graduation, be debarred from receiving a Diploma; if at any annual examination other than his final, or at any intermediate examination, he will be rusticated, and, in addition, lose all the marks given for that particular paper, and will not be re-examined in it.

In Billy's case that meant being set back a year. He was re-admitted for 1912–13, but condemned to repeat his first year. The second time around, the advantages that accrued from repetition enabled him to place twenty-third out of forty-two — quite a respectable showing. In his second year, 1913–14, however, he was back at the bottom of the class: thirty-third out of thirty-four. The one cadet below him failed his year.

Having completed their third year, Billy's original classmates graduated in the spring of 1914 and produced, at their own expense, the usual class yearbook. Despite the fact that two years had now passed since he had taken classes with them, Billy was included in it (did he pay his share, or was his inclusion entirely a tribute to his charm and popularity among his one-time peers?), and the entry devoted to him perhaps illustrates one aspect of his academic problems. Girls — and, in this case, probably not Margaret Burden!

> Voice from Cadet with telescope peering out of his window: "There's a red coat on Fort Henry hill. There's an umbrella there, too, with a couple of people behind it. Wonder who it can be?"
> Voice from next room: "Come on, Steve, Bill Bish is out, let's swipe his tobacco."[2]

Bishop returned to RMC for his graduating year on 28 August 1914, just twenty-four days after Great Britain had declared war on Germany and automatically taken her colonies, including Canada, with her. It was a popular decision among Canada's anglophone communities, however, and young, single men with a romantic, idealized view of war stampeded to the Colours. Bishop must have been torn as to which direction to take. Although enrolled at a military institution, we have his own word for it that "I had never given much thought to being a soldier,"[3] and he was certainly not the sort who would happily tolerate the kinds of physical hardship indivisible from much of early twentieth-century soldiering. He must have had some inkling of those hardships; on the other hand, he probably also recognized that joining the army would relieve him from his academic travails. For the moment, however, he did nothing.

It was customary for the senior class to supply most of the cadet appointments within the college, such cadet non-commissioned officers being selected by the commandant largely on the advice of his adjutant. Surprisingly, given his disciplinary and academic record and the qualities expected of cadet NCOs, Bishop was appointed a lance corporal and, ten days later, promoted to corporal. "Cadets so entrusted with authority should remember that upon their example and the manner in which their duties are performed, in a great measure depend the general conduct, gentleman-like, honourable and moral tone of the cadets," intoned Standing Orders.[4] There was little in his college record to date to suggest that he was likely to set such an example to his juniors, but it seems young Billy could charm commandants and adjutants as well as girls.

On 16 September, fifteen of Bishop's classmates left the college, having accepted commissions in the British Army. A sixteenth soon departed in search of a Canadian Militia commission, and at the end of the month Billy, too, withdrew "at parents' request," the time-honoured formula for escaping without a diploma on the one hand or expulsion on the other. On a scale of Exemplary, Very Good, Good or Bad — the last one reserved for cadets who were expelled — his discharge certificate assessed his conduct as "Good."

He was immediately commissioned in the Mississauga Horse, a well-entrenched and fashionable Toronto militia regiment, but the whimsical, egocentric ideas of Canada's minister of militia and defence, Sam Hughes, meant that the unit would never be mobilized for active service. Instead, numbered battalions and regiments were being created out of thin air to form the Canadian Expeditionary Force, an approach which at least ensured that there would be no bitter recriminations (with inevitable political undertones, since the "militia colonels" constituted a powerful parliamentary lobby) between units selected for overseas service and those condemned to remain at home.

The First Contingent was preparing to leave for England and a Second Contingent was now forming. There was no glory to be won serving in Canada, and Billy desperately needed glory to impress the

Burdens as a potential son-in-law. He transferred to one of Hughes' creations, the 7th Canadian Mounted Rifles, which was mobilizing for active service in London, Ontario. Its commanding officer, Lieutenant Colonel Ibbotson Leonard, a thirty-three-year-old businessman, had graduated from RMC in brother Worth's year, 1903 (now and later, Dame Fortune often smiled on Billy Bishop). Bishop, a fellow alumnus if not a fellow graduate, and a fine rider to boot, quickly established himself as one of Leonard's favourites. The latter's diary records how often Billy was at his home for lunch, tea or dinner, and later at his lodgings near Folkestone, England.[5]

Meanwhile, in France and Flanders, barbed wire and machine guns were already dominating the battlefield, while poison gas was beginning to play a part. There would be no significant role for cavalrymen in this war. The already-formed first two brigades of Canadian Mounted Rifles, all six regiments, were dismounted and turned into four battalions of infantry, which became the 8th Brigade of the 3rd Canadian Division. The 7th CMR, originally intended for a third mounted brigade, was broken up, one squadron (handpicked by Leonard, who, through his friendship with Sam Hughes, retained command of it while preserving his lieutenant colonel's rank) keeping its horses and becoming the 2nd Division's mounted reconnaissance squadron.[*] Bishop, appointed a troop leader, was among the five officers chosen by Leonard to stay with him, and the squadron sailed from Montreal aboard the *Caledonian* on 9 June 1915, arriving in England on the 22nd. He was off to war, to do his duty for King and country! Before he left, he became informally engaged to Margaret Burden. Now all he needed to do was convince her parents that he was worthy of their daughter.

---

[*] The remainder of the regiment eventually became the Canadian Cavalry Depot in England, handling reinforcements and postings for the Canadian Cavalry Brigade in France.

By early July, the squadron was under canvas at Dibgate, near Folkestone, on England's south coast, and Bishop was complaining bitterly about the dust storms that beset the camp. "You can't imagine what we are going through here today," he wrote in a letter to Margaret.

> A frightful sandstorm is on. It is so bad one can barely breathe, and outside cannot dare open one's eyes. Even goggles are no protection, the fine sand gets in. Our eyes are full of blood, and the sand is so bad that some of the men's faces are bleeding. We have had to cut out all parades, and only leave our tents to tighten up the guys and tend to the poor horses. They are suffering awfully, poor dumb things. I have just been out to see mine and they all nuzzled up to me trying their level best to talk.... As I write this sand floats over the paper every minute and I have to keep blowing it off.

Two days later:

> Yesterday it rained all afternoon and evening and night, and we rode through it, leaving here at 2 p.m. and getting back at 1 this morning. It would have been a lovely ride if the weather had been decent, but it wasn't half bad as it was, although we all got soaked and this morning woke up with nasty colds. It is still raining and we are, of course, still soaking wet.

When it wasn't raining, it was blowing hard. On the 14th, "today we are faced with another sandstorm which is blowing everything to pieces," and the next day, although the sandstorm was over:

35

... streams of thunderstorms come down on us. We are planning to march out on a bivouac this afternoon and come back tomorrow afternoon, but owing to the awful weather conditions we may not do it. I hope not, as sleeping in wet grass is no fun, but I am afraid we will go in spite of all.[6]

"Streams of thunderstorms," indeed. Letter after letter complains about the weather, although the official history of the Canadian Expeditionary Force makes a point of noting that, unlike the previous year, "it was a dry summer, and life under canvas presented no hardship."[7] Not for most men, perhaps, but it did for Bishop. He was briefly in hospital when "the chill I got on our bivouac knocked me partially out of working order, and as a tent is a poor place to get over a chill they sent me here for a few days."[8] His medical documents called it pleurisy.[9]

There were wounded officers in the hospital, back from the newly congealed Western Front, and no doubt Bishop learned from them how much worse the best of trench life could be. Much worse than Dibgate. Wetter and colder and muddier — not to mention the rats! Returning to duty after a few days in hospital, and visiting Folkestone, he fell into conversation with an unidentified staff officer and heard about the rather easier life of an airman in France, with a jovial mess to relax in of an evening, and a comfortable bed to lie on at night. Not a bit like the trenches. Bishop did not fear danger, although he had yet to experience it in any degree: it was discomfort that repelled him, and he must have made that clear to his new acquaintance.

I got a note from an officer yesterday on the staff of the Royal Flying Corps whom I had met in Folkestone, asking me to call on him at the War Office today [6

August 1915]. I had no idea what it was about but came hot foot, as a summons to the W.O. is something to make a poor subaltern tremble. Anyway, I went to see him and he enlightened me to the following extent. There is a vacancy in the RFC for an observing officer (there are two kinds, pilots and observing officers) and he offered it to me — if I can get transferred from the Canadians. I am to call again at 12.45 tomorrow and see Lord Cecil, whoever he is, he has something to do with it, and will know more then. It is a great chance, as everybody is merely watching for such an opportunity.[10]

He was interviewed by Lieutenant Lord Hugh Cecil, the staff officer in charge of aircrew recruiting, whose wartime rank in the army belied his status in society. Cecil was the balding, witty, middle-aged son of former prime minister Lord Salisbury, brother of the current earl, and he promptly offered Bishop a transfer to the RFC as an observer "just as soon as I can get my application through Canadian Divisional HQ."[11]

Colonel Leonard was agreeable, all went well, and on 1 September 1915, Bishop joined a newly formed 21 Squadron at Netheravon, on Salisbury Plain, to be trained as an observer. On the 4th came his first flight, when he was taken up in an Avro 504. He told Margaret Burden that "at a height of 3,000 feet it was glorious and I enjoyed every minute of it. There is certainly no sport like it in the world. Rushing along about 80 miles an hour, away up so that people look like mere specks.... It must be wonderful up about 12,000 feet."[12] There was a pardonable but typical degree of exaggeration in his estimate of the speed at which he had flown — the Avro's top speed was only 62 mph. Three days later, he was even more wound up. "This is the greatest game in the world, every minute of it full of intense excitement. A man ceases to be human when he is away up. The earth is merely a map and you feel that nothing is impossible."[13]

The squadron was breaking in the new RE 7, a stable but mechanically unreliable two-seater biplane in which the observer-gunner occupied the front cockpit, the pilot the rear one. No regular defensive armament was fitted, but the observer-gunner was usually equipped with a drum-fed Lewis gun. Given Bishop's later prowess with the Lewis, one would like to know how he did in his initial firing practices, but he made no mention of that aspect of his training in his letters. "I had two good flights with Rutledge [his pilot] this morning. We went out to take photographs of certain places ... and had the most wonderful luck with them, so much so that the adjutant is sending some of mine to the War Office as an example of the photography here." On 11 November: "I was put in charge of all the observers for the 4th Wing. It is a promotion but a rotten job, as I have to train all the new observers coming in and lecture, etc., which being rotten at I heartily hate." A week later, "the Colonel told me a favourable report on my work [on artillery co-operation] had come from Lark Hill."[14]

On 24 November, Billy Bishop was involved in his first crash. The fuselages of most aircraft at that time were constructed entirely of wood, but the front end of the RE 7 was built up on a steel tube box girder which offered some protection to the crew against a frontal impact. "Both of us got off very lightly, I got my foot bruised a bit and now have a very artistic limp of which I am very proud. The pilot was also very lucky and only got a few little bruises."

The experience did nothing to deter him from flying. Indeed, three days later, "I had what was probably the most thrilling time of my life."

I flew over to the Central Flying School [at nearby Upavon] with one of the instructors there, and a new machine had just come in and had to be tested, so up we went in it.... We went up to 13,000 feet and dove straight down for 11,000 ft.* When we flattened out we were going about 300 miles an hour, so you may imagine the sensation to see the earth approaching you at that rate. Then we flew up again and got the machine facing vertically upward, and shut off the engine. She came down backwards about 300 ft. and then he righted her again. Then he looped the loop, after that he banked her up vertical and we side-slipped about 1,000 ft. Then we came down.[15]

Again, he was exaggerating the speed, this time quite substantially. In 1915 there was nothing on the drawing boards capable of reaching speeds anywhere near 300 mph, even in a dive. He was almost certainly in a Sopwith 1-1/2 Strutter, a stoutly built fighter-reconnaissance biplane, which made its first official appearance in December 1915. It might — just *might* — have been able to reach 160 mph in a dive without the wings being torn off. Such exaggerations were relatively inconsequential in themselves, but they do confirm that Bishop was not much concerned with truth in principle. A good story was far more important.

When Colonel Leonard took his squadron of cavalry to France with the 2nd Division in September 1915, Bishop was still undergoing

---

* Metrification had not yet raised its ugly head in the English-speaking world, and this book — like Bishop and his peers — will use the Imperial system of weights and measures.

observer training with the RFC. The pretty and charming Mrs. Leonard stayed in England where, she reported to her husband, Bishop was squiring her about town. Leonard's diary records that "Sarah saw Billy in London on Sat[urday]," and, a week later, that "Sarah who was in London ... had dinner with Billy and went to the theatre. Don't like it." There is no suggestion of an intimate relationship, but gossip was a mainstay of Canadian society in the United Kingdom. It would hardly have been considered appropriate for a young, attractive colonel's lady to be seen gadding about the capital — not with her husband, but with a good-looking young subaltern in tow. Two days later, Leonard "wrote Sarah about Billy," presumably to point that out to her and warn her to be more prudent. Still, the matter apparently did not affect his old relationship with Bishop. When the latter arrived in France, Leonard quickly had him "in for dinner" again.[16]

On 18 January 1916, Number 21 Squadron, including Bishop, went to France by sea. Had he stayed with Leonard and the divisional cavalry squadron, he would have got there three months earlier, and therein hangs a tale that says much about him. Only those officers and men who saw service in a theatre of war before 31 December 1915 would subsequently be entitled to wear the 1914–1915 Star. That meant, of course, that Bishop's former comrades in the cavalry made the cut, while he missed out by a matter of two and a half weeks. A form letter in his National Archives of Canada file confirms as much, listing the various campaign medals he was entitled to as a member of the Canadian Expeditionary Force and as an officer of the RFC and RAF. Both British and Canadian authorities crossed out the 1914–1915 Star while acknowledging that he was eligible for the British War Medal and the Victory Medal.[17] However, an examination of his tunic, now in the hands of the Canadian War Museum, reveals a "red, white and blue, shaded and watered" ribbon in the appropriate place among the multitude of medals that adorn it. At some point in his later career, Bishop unobtrusively awarded himself the 1914–1915 Star!

Days after its arrival in France, 21 Squadron became the first unit in the field to be equipped with the RE 7, which was theoretically capable of lifting a 336-pound bomb as well as pilot and observer. In practice, however, it was often incapable of such effort. Indeed, it was sometimes incapable of lifting itself, the engine being quite unreliable. "I am of the opinion that the RE 7 with 120 hp Beardmore engine is useless in the field," wrote Major General Hugh Trenchard, the RFC commander in France. "The lifting power of the machine rapidly decreases, and … the fact remains that not half the machines can get off the ground if it is at all sticky with full load, nor can they climb to 8,000 ft. Therefore, I shall be glad to have these machines replaced at an early date."[18] At the other end of the spectrum, Second Lieutenant J.B. Brophy, another Canadian, who would join 21 Squadron only days after Bishop left and who would subsequently be killed in a flying accident on Christmas Eve 1916, noted in his diary that "everyone hates them, and all agreed that anyone who crosses the lines in one should be awarded the Military Cross."[19]

In the spring of 1916 all flying machines were dangerous, but some more so than others, and in the latter category the RE 7 may have been pre-eminent. The stress of simply flying in one must have been tremendous, made all the worse for those observers placing themselves entirely in the hands of another man when structural or mechanical problems — not to mention human error — arose. Bishop endured his share of crash landings during the three and a half months he was in France with 21 Squadron, but was not unduly affected by them and apparently did a sound job of work. On one occasion he was grazed by a piece of antiaircraft shrapnel. His son describes it as "only a slight bruise on the side of the head,"[20] but despite the absence of blood, if Arthur's description is true it apparently entitled Billy to a wound stripe — a short, narrow, vertical bar of gold thread worn on his left sleeve. Or was his wound stripe as questionable as his 1914–1915 Star?

He also claimed to have injured his knee in a crash landing — not severely enough to send him to hospital at the time, but enough to prove a lingering problem which was to be exacerbated when he went on leave. Other misfortunes beset him on the ground, according to Arthur. On one occasion he was driving an RFC tender (a sort of early station wagon-cum-light truck) that collided with another vehicle and left him severely shaken up; on another, a blow to the head incurred in a hangar accident allegedly left him unconscious for two days. There is no mention of any of these misfortunes in his medical records, although an infected tooth put him in hospital for a week.[21]

When his turn for leave came around, at the beginning of May 1916, he was physically exhausted and his nerves were at breaking point. He told Margaret:

> … in the air you feel only intense excitement. You cheer and laugh and keep your spirits up. You are all right just after you have landed as you search your machine for bullet and shrapnel holes. But two hours later when you are quietly sitting in your billet you feel a sudden loneliness. You want to lie down and cry.[22]

Classic symptoms of combat fatigue.

Disembarking from the Channel ferry at Folkestone, Bishop allegedly stumbled and fell, re-injuring his knee; but, determined to enjoy his leave despite the pain, he struggled on until it came time to return to France. Then, and only then, did he go to the RFC hospital in Bryanston Square, where (again, according to Arthur) the doctors found that he had "a severely strained heart" in addition to his knee injury.[23] On the surface, heart trouble seems unlikely, for there was no history of it, nor would his heart apparently ever trouble him when he returned to the front. After one later flight, in which he reached 18,500 feet without supplementary oxygen, he did complain, but only to say that "my head and lungs were bursting"[24] — a very reasonable reaction in the circumstances. No mention of his heart. In *Winged Warfare*, he attributes his "several months" of hospitalization and convalescence to his knee injury. However, his medical history only records "varicose veins, both legs"[25] — not nearly as romantic as a strained heart or a gimpy knee.

A few days after his admission to hospital, Bishop awoke from an afternoon nap to find an elderly woman who was a total stranger at his bedside. She introduced herself as Lady St. Helier, busy succouring the sick and wounded as a volunteer. She was destined to play a significant part in Bishop's spectacular rise to fame and fortune. Born Susan Mary Stewart-Mackenzie of Seaforth, in 1849, she was related to half the Highland chieftains of Scotland and was the wealthy widow of a probate court judge, having buried another rich husband before him. Clever, charming and vivacious,

> [s]he had a rare double gift: she could make close friends and keep them, and at the same time she could attract new people, people of mark, many of them birds of passage.... Many of her best friends were among the politicians, not only of one party: Of

these Lord Randolph Churchill [Winston's father and a prominent Conservative, died 1895] and Mr. W.E. Forster [a prominent Liberal, died 1886] may be named in the front rank....

As to the general society that gathered in her house, it can only be summed up in the word "everybody." Bishops and Ambassadors (especially American), Cabinet Ministers and Opposition, Judges and lawyers in abundance ... editors, journalists, historians, women pretty or clever or both — all were there and all were glad to come again.[26]

Not the least of St. Helier's friends was Princess Marie Louise, the daughter of the self-exiled Prince Christian of Schleswig-Holstein (whose claims on that province had been effectively extinguished when it fell into Prussian hands via the Peace of Vienna in 1864) and Queen Victoria's third daughter, Princess Helena — a relationship that made her a first cousin to King George V. Another was Winston Churchill, for the moment out of office but formerly Home Secretary (1910) and First Lord of the Admiralty (1911), and shortly to become Lloyd George's minister of munitions. Churchill's wife, the former Clementine Hozier, was St. Helier's great-niece. She claimed to have introduced them, and the Churchills' wedding reception had certainly been held at her home in Portland Place, when Lord Hugh Cecil, the venerable lieutenant who had interviewed Bishop at the War Office, had been Churchill's best man. Cecil held one of the two Oxford University seats in the House of Commons, his title being an honorary one since he was a younger son.

Other influential confidantes included the brilliant jurist F.E. Smith, currently attorney general in the Lloyd George administration and, as Earl of Birkenhead, the future Lord Chancellor of England. Mary St. Helier welcomed to her house every member of the Cabinet, starting with the prime minister, and invitations were eagerly sought. She was probably the most influential hostess in London in an era when "half the policy of England was settled at dinner parties and social gatherings."[27]

According to Arthur Bishop, she had seen Billy's name on the hospital register, "and I was sure that someone named William Bishop, from Canada, *must* be the son of my friend Will Bishop."[28] She went on to explain that she had once met his father at a reception given by the Canadian prime minister, Sir Wilfrid Laurier. When was that? It could not have been later than October 1911, when Laurier left office, and country lawyer Will Bishop was hardly a socially or politically significant Canadian, nor a charismatic personality. Yet, at the very least, more than five years later she remembered him from among a cast of hundreds, if the story is true. But the ultimate causes of the Bishop–St. Helier meeting are unimportant. What matters is that this cosmopolitan blueblood, whose only son had died of typhoid in India in 1904, aged twenty-two, virtually adopted the mannerly, good-looking twenty-two-year-old Canadian as an honorary grandson. When Bishop left hospital he was taken into her home to convalesce; and when he learned that his father had suffered a slight stroke, it was "Granny" St. Helier who pulled the strings that got him a leave to Canada — a rare privilege for an inconsequential subaltern who had been overseas less than a year.

That furlough enabled Bishop to become formally engaged to Margaret Burden, but was otherwise uneventful. Early in September 1916 he returned to England, only to find his application for pilot training ignored — whether for medical or administrative reasons is not clear. Lady St. Helier, a puppet-mistress if ever there was one, apparently pulled more strings to get him accepted.

His experience as an observer stood him in good stead during ground training at the School of Military Aeronautics, and "by special permission [I] was allowed to take my examination three weeks earlier than would have been the case in the ordinary course of events. I worked like a Trojan, and passed without much difficulty."[29] What a change from RMC! Off he went, to Upavon, on Salisbury Plain, where he learned to fly a Maurice Farman Série 11 (known colloquially as a Rumpity), which boasted an 80 hp Renault engine and a maximum speed of 72 mph. The fuselage consisted of an open framework of wooden spars with an enclosed nacelle for pilot and student set just under the upper wing and well above the lower one. It looked exceedingly delicate but was in fact a "quite workmanlike" aircraft for the time.[30]

It was physically much harder to fly those primitive machines, in which the hazardous relationship between muscle and mechanism was direct and elementary, than a modern jet with its fly-by-wire controls, computers, and multitudinous electronic checks and balances. "In practically no other acquired accomplishment has man to keep so many groups of antagonistic muscles in a state of static wakefulness, or to perform such variety of constant co-ordinated leg and arm movements," wrote an early flight surgeon who was also a pilot and thus knew whereof he spoke. "The successful flyer must be one who has the power to co-ordinate his limb muscles with a beautiful degree of refinement ..."[31]

Bishop would surely have agreed with that assessment.

> Never will I forget those days of dual control. I tried very hard, but it seemed to me I just could not get the proper "feel" of the machine. First the instructor would tell me I was "ham-handed" — that I gripped the controls too tightly with every muscle tense. After

that I would get what you might call timid-handed, and not hold the controls tightly enough. My instructor and I both suffered tortures.[32]

Nevertheless, he proved to be a rather better-than-average pupil, soloing after only three hours of dual instruction. That may have been more a reflection of his self-confidence than his real ability, and it may well have been that same self-confidence that enabled him to do well enough at night flying to win a posting to a night fighter squadron defending London. Leefe Robinson had just been awarded his Victoria Cross for shooting down Zeppelin *SL 11*, and perhaps Bishop already had his eye on something similar. "I was very anxious to get taken on for this work, and eventually succeeded."[33] He went to 11 Squadron at Hendon for specialized training.

Night flying, at least on a moonless or cloudy night, was inconceivably more difficult. The only instruments were a compass, an altimeter, an airspeed indicator and a lateral inclinometer with a "bubble," which served as a rudimentary turn-and-bank indicator. Without adequate instrumentation, pilots were required to fly "by the seat of their pants" — an exercise that, despite the nature of the metaphor, demanded an extraordinary determination to reject physical impressions on occasion in favour of some higher, intuitive, understanding of what was happening.

> Night flying is a fearsome thing — but tremendously interesting. Any one who has ever been swimming at night will appreciate what I mean. All the familiar objects and landmarks that seem so friendly by day, become weird and repellent monsters at night....
>
> I could not see a thing around me; only the stars overhead. After flying straight-away for several min-

utes I summoned up courage enough to make a
turn. I carefully and gradually rounded the corner,
and the away off to one side I could see the flares on
the ground....

Whenever I had to make a turn I made a very
gradual one, hardly daring to bank, or tilt my machine
at all. It is funny, this feeling at night that you must not
bank, and a most dangerous instinct to follow.[34]

In early December 1916, Bishop was posted to 37 Squadron,
formed three months earlier as a Home Defence unit to cover
northeast London. The squadron was equipped with a mixture of
BE 12a's and FE 2b's, and he was assigned to a BE, the better
machine of the two for anti-Zeppelin purposes since it had a slightly higher operational ceiling. It was too stable for effective dogfight-
ing and therefore a failure in France, but stability was no problem
while chasing airships, and perhaps made it easier to fly by night.

Bishop went to the two-pilot detachment flying out of Sutton's
Farm, near Southend, on the north shore of the Thames estuary,
the likeliest approach route for a Zeppelin since the shorelines
provided an infallible guide to London on even the darkest nights:
lights on the shore side, pitch blackness on the seaward side. But
the success of Leefe Robinson, using the new incendiary ammunition and achieved at the extraordinary height (for the time) of
around 12,000 feet, together with the accidental loss of two more
airships on the night of 23–24 September, was causing the
Germans to rethink their airship strategy. While they did so, the
raids ceased and there were no attacks on London during Bishop's
time with 37 Squadron. "My luck as a Zeppelin hunter was very
poor," he wrote. "I used to dream occasionally about stalking the
great monsters in the high thin air, pouring a drum of blazing bul-

lets into them and gloating as they flared into flame. But no real Zeppelins ever came my way."[35]

Much has been made of Bishop's allegedly meagre flying skills (not least by his son) and it is true that he sometimes exhibited a tendency to make landings that approached the category of controlled crashes. However, the fact that he had been posted to a Home Defence squadron, with its emphasis on difficult night flying, *and* that he survived three months of it without a serious mishap, suggests he was not as bad a pilot as he has been painted. A good number of men in the eleven Home Defence squadrons that guarded the east coast of England in 1917 did manage to kill or seriously injure themselves in flying accidents while Bishop survived unscathed.

While with 37 Squadron at Sutton's Farm, Bishop fought his first, but not his last, imaginary combat. W.D. Mathieson, in his *Billy Bishop, VC*, quotes a letter that he wrote home, one which is not included in the correspondence deposited with the Department of National Defence.

January 7th [1917] I had such an exciting time. I spent the day taking mechanics for joyrides, and then just about noon a Hun seaplane toddled over, and Headquarters ordered me to go up after him.

I did and caught up to him at 1,000 feet and had a terrific scrap.... He had an observer and I was alone but I was in a BE 12a and it is very fast. I must have hit him over and over again but didn't finish him. He hit my machine 6 times — 3 times, funny to say, in the propeller.[36]

A photocopy of Bishop's logbook is in the Bishop biographical file at the Directorate of History and Heritage, and it makes no mention of any such incident. Six joyrides for mechanics are recorded in the entry for 7 January, together with one ten-minute flight for unspecified reasons — probably some kind of flight test. Nor is it a matter of some slight misdating. There is no account of any meeting with a hostile machine during his stay with 37 Squadron — not even a suggestion of one — but no doubt the story impressed his correspondent. On 22 January 1917, he told Margaret Burden that he had been recommended for command of a flight and, according to him, the recommendation was repeated at the end of February.[37] However, there is no other evidence of that and it is hard to understand why he should have been thus selected. There were much better qualified pilots — who had seen service in France — available to fill any such vacancy.

London was within easy reach of Sutton's Farm, and when in town he stayed with Lady St. Helier. One wonders if any other Owen Sound lad of his generation could have carried off luncheon and dinner parties, *thé dansants* and soirées, with the charming insouciance that Bishop must have displayed. Did he cultivate his slight lisp, à la Winston Churchill? Miss Pearl's dance classes were paying off in spades, but there was business as well as pleasure in the social whirl. No doubt it was "Granny" who arranged for him to dine with Captain Albert Ball, "the man who has 3 DSOs and 2 MCs and a foreign order."[38]* Ball had been posted home for a rest and was unhappily employed on instructional duties while he struggled to get a posting back to France. Bishop was properly, even overly, impressed, perhaps dreaming that he might one day display such a row of ribbons.

Bishop's supplications to get to France must have included a request to go to one of the new, specialized fighter squadrons that were

---

* He had, in reality, two DSOs, one MC, and a *Croix de Guerre*!

now being formed, for in mid-February he was posted back to the Central Flying School for a short course on the Sopwith Pup, at that time one of three barely adequate fighters in the RFC inventory. It was, of course, typical of service bureaucracy that when he did get to France he would be posted to a squadron flying one of the other types.

He also put in some time instructing on Avro 504s, "a machine I hate."

> Yesterday I had 3 forced landings on them, 2 of which I managed to get into the aerodrome, but the last one I crashed on the side of a hill, not very badly, nobody was hurt and the machine is repairable. The engines are so very unreliable in them.... Today I had better luck and managed to get several pupils ready for their first "solo."
>
> Last night we had a boy killed here and another in my squadron this morning. I saw them both, perfectly ghastly sights. The one today was on a Sopwith. He was diving it and the wings fell off.... The thing fell like a stone 3,000 feet, the poor beggar struggling all the time, helpless. Then they killed a pupil at Netheravon today also, so we aren't doing badly, are we?
>
> Those things used to upset me so horribly, but now I think I have become an absolute firmly believing fatalist and they don't worry my nerve in the least. If I am for it, then I am, and nothing can save me; but I firmly believe I am NOT for it.[39]

That was a useful philosophy to carry across the English Channel, with RFC casualties rising steadily and "bloody April" in the offing. On a more practical level, the extra flying time that he had put in, first as an observer and then as a pilot, gave him a much better chance of surviving what was to come than the average novice posted straight from flying school to a front-line squadron. Perhaps the most difficult part of becoming a successful fighter pilot lay in learning what to look for, and how to look for it, in order to avoid being surprised by an opponent. These were skills that could only be mastered through experience. In the spring of 1917, not many pilots lived long enough to gain that key experience.

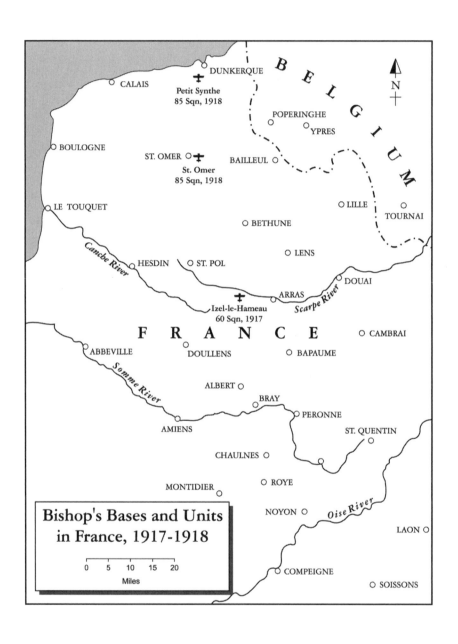

Bishop's Bases and Units in France, 1917-1918

Miles
0　5　10　15　20

CHAPTER 2

A Pilot at the Front

On 9 March 1917, the day after Major Evelyn Graves, the squadron's crippled (as the result of an earlier flying accident) commanding officer, had been shot down in flames and killed, Bishop joined 60 Squadron, RFC, at Filescamp Farm, just outside the village of Izel-le-Hameau, some eight miles west of Arras and eleven miles west of the front line. Arthur Lee, who joined the squadron later that year, set the scene.

> A vast aerodrome in open countryside, with accommodation for three squadrons.... Our quarters are most civilized, as we have a pleasant Mess, Nissen huts for officers and N[on] C[ommissioned] O[ffi-cer]s, a hard tennis court of sorts, and a badminton court in an empty hangar next door. And all this sited in a large orchard full of luscious fruit trees.[1]

Foul weather prevented any flying on the 10th, and Bishop spent the day getting acquainted with his new comrades, who were mourning Graves' loss — one among six the squadron had experienced over the past two weeks.* But there was no great pause in the fighting; the next morning, Bishop and another replacement pilot watched patrols leaving for missions over the front.

Using two sticks, Graves' successor, Jack Scott, hobbled awkwardly into the squadron office that afternoon. Like Lady St. Helier, Scott had many close allies in the interlocking cliques of Whitehall and Mayfair that revolved around school, club and Parliament, and he, too, was destined to play a key role in building the Bishop legend. Assessing his former commanding officer from the perspective of old age, Wing Commander W.M. (Willie) Fry, Bishop's contemporary in 60 Squadron, commented that:

> [h]e was the third lame C[ommanding] O[fficer] in succession,** a man of character and presence, a barrister, Sussex squire and fox-hunting man with a host of friends, many in high places. He was obviously ambitious and determined that the squadron should be the best in France. He was the first commanding officer I had served under who was what today would be described as public-relations minded .... He was determined that his squadron's and his pilots' deeds should be known by all and sundry, and he was generous in recommending for honours pilots who did well.[2]

---

* Since the squadron establishment was eighteen pilots, this was a 33 per cent loss rate.

** All three were the result of flying accidents. The first, Robert Smith-Barry, would form and command the School of Special Flying at Gosport, in August 1917. There he would re-define and rationalize the whole concept of flying training, a process that would save a great many lives over the next year and on into the peacetime era.

Pure luck brought Bishop into Scott's orbit at a time when there was a desperate need on the part of government and the army to make the most of any gleam of talent and turn RFC geese into swans.

Scott was the son of a wealthy New Zealander, Henry Alan Scott, who had left his native heath in 1872 to take a law degree in England and then practise from chambers in London's Inner Temple, the hub of English jurisprudence. He returned to New Zealand to marry in 1881, and the following year Alan John — always known as Jack — was born. Subsequently, the family returned to England, settling in London (Chelsea) in time for Jack to attend a German high school in Hannover for three years and then complete his education by taking a Fourth in History — an academic idler's degree — at Merton College, Oxford, between 1903 and 1907.[3]

His sporting and social life flourished, however, and he became Master of the University Draghounds, an expensive distinction that ensured he would mix with many eminent characters both within and without the Oxford community. One of them was the rising jurist and parliamentarian F.E. Smith, soon to be attorney general, who was noted for his pugnacious personality and witty tongue. Smith was a Fellow of Merton and a keen rider to hounds, so that his and Scott's paths inevitably crossed, and he was greatly impressed with young Jack. "I never saw anyone, in my long experience of the hunting field, ride with a resolution and fearlessness so complete," he later wrote in Scott's obituary for *The Times*. "Acquaintance ripened rapidly into friendship."[4]

Following in his father's footsteps, and no doubt encouraged by Smith, Scott read for the law after leaving Merton. By 1911, he was practising at the South London sessions and on the South-East circuit from his father's old address in the Inner Temple.[5] Two years earlier, he had obtained a commission in the Sussex Yeomanry, a fashionable militia cavalry regiment, but he was apparently not that keen an amateur soldier, for in 1912 he resigned his commission.[6]

The threat of war brought him back to the Yeomanry in 1914, but he was quick to realize that there was little prospect of horse soldiers seeing much action. Anxious to find a more challenging aspect of war, Scott turned to the Royal Flying Corps, where the ability to ride well was considered to be a great asset in potential pilots. That was not as foolish as it may sound: to ride well demands — and develops — a fine sense of balance, an essential skill in the early days of flying.

"He had never in his life been in an aeroplane; he was over thirty years old; but the air, and the prospect of air fighting, made an irresistible appeal to his adventurous nature," recalled Smith.[7] Another of Smith's good friends, a prominent politician, was also learning to fly, with rather less success, at the ripe old age of forty,* and had they not been friends before, Scott and Winston Churchill became so then.

It was Scott's misfortune that "before he went to France his machine collapsed when he was 2,000 ft in the air … when some 60 ft from the ground he regained a degree of control which saved his life but left him permanently a cripple."[8] Despite his injuries, Scott clung to his commission and was subsequently posted to a desk job at RFC Headquarters, in those early days of the war still occupying De Keyser's Hotel in London's West End. From there he wheedled his way onto a squadron working up to operational standards under Major Sholto Douglas (who would finish his service career as a marshal of the Royal Air Force).

---

* At the time Churchill was First Lord of the Admiralty and pressure of work soon compelled him to abandon flying lessons. Shortly after the war ended he was taking lessons again, but 'though he flies many hours, he never aquires the "air sense" essential to a good pilot. The inevitable crash comes at last. Churchill, as usual, escapes unhurt, but his instructor, the brave Jack Scott … again suffers serious injuries." — "Ephesian", [Carl Roberts] Winston Churchill (London, Mills and Boon, 1927), p 215.

At first I felt rather awkward about giving orders to this thirty-five year old who was obviously a man of the world. I felt that such orders coming from a whipper-snapper of only just twenty-three years of age might be resented; but Jack Scott was to teach me a very good lesson both in the balance of maturity and the handling of men.[9]

Soon Scott "began again to strain every influence he possessed to obtain leave to go on active service." His mentor, Smith, tried desperately to stop him, actually borrowing his medical file from a co-operative doctor and showing it to Sir David Henderson, the Director of Military Training at the War Office and senior officer of the RFC, so that Henderson could see for himself how physically impaired Scott was. It was all to no avail. "For the moment I succeeded, but a month later he came round to our house, the embodiment of gaiety, and told us he was under orders to proceed to France to take command of a squadron in the following week."[10]

First, however, Scott needed to familiarize himself with conditions at the front. Initially he went to France as a flight commander in 43 Squadron, equipped with the new Sopwith 1-1/2 Strutter. Although he was not credited with any victories during his brief stint with Number 43 ("He was never a good pilot, but was a most determined air fighter"[11]), Major General Hugh Trenchard, the general officer commanding (GOC) the RFC in France, was keeping a solicitous eye on him. When Graves was killed, Scott was promoted to succeed him in command of 60 Squadron.

It is clear that Scott's charisma and determination were key factors in all this, but there was also a delicate and subtle bond between Trenchard and Scott that may well have played a part. Trenchard went back to London on service business from time to time, and as the RFC was still a very small organization and staffs not nearly as lavish as they have since become, he could scarcely have failed to notice the disabled officer dragging himself about headquarters on crutches. In South Africa sixteen years earlier, Trenchard, too, had been "half-paralyzed from the waist downwards," and had lost the use of his legs for some months as the result of a bullet wound. Believing the impairment to be permanent, he had struggled desperately to overcome it until a lucky accident had unexpectedly wrenched a vertebra back into place, taken pressure off his spinal cord, and restored his mobility.[12] Consequently, he above all people could hardly fail to sympathize with Scott. It was the kind of tie that binds, irrespective of rank.

Number 60 Squadron was part of III Brigade, RFC, commanded by Colonel (Acting Brigadier General) J.F.A. Higgins, which was, in turn, part of the British Expeditionary Force's Third Army* under General Sir Edmund Allenby. A pre-war Regular soldier, the monocled, debonair Higgins, third on the RFC's seniority list behind Henderson and Trenchard and with a DSO from South Africa, had been something of a military man-about-town in pre-war London, mixing easily in the same circles as Scott, Smith, the Churchills, Lady St. Helier and the like. His brigade consisted of two wings: 12th (Corps) Wing with four squadrons of two-seaters, primarily employed in supporting ground troops; and 13th (Army) Wing, with four squadrons of "scouts" (as First World War fighters were commonly called) busy struggling for air superiority.

The 13th Wing, to which 60 Squadron belonged, was commanded by twenty-six-year-old Lieutenant Colonel George F. Pretyman, another professional soldier, who had been seconded to

---

* Each of the BEF's armies had an RFC brigade as an integral part of it.

the RFC in 1914. The son of a major general, he had been awarded a DSO in March 1915 for "great gallantry, ability and initiative on numerous occasions" with the RFC in France. Only four years older than Bishop, he soon became as much a friend as a superior, and he, too, would prove to be an enthusiastic booster of the Canadian. In the Bishop correspondence, Pretyman is usually referred to simply as "the Colonel," just as Higgins is "the General." Yet another in this intricate web of friendship and influence that would further Bishop's career was Allenby's military secretary, Lieutenant Colonel Lord Dalmeny, Grenadier Guards, the eldest son of another former prime minister, the Earl of Rosebery.

Number 60 Squadron's business lay in patrolling, and hopefully controlling, the air above Vimy Ridge. It was also expected, as part of Trenchard's offensive strategy, to dominate German air space as far to the east — ten or twelve miles — as it could reasonably reach. Together with four other RFC squadrons on the Western Front, Number 60 was equipped with French-built Nieuport 17 biplanes, most of them the C 1 variant. They were not as fast in level flight as their most frequent opponent in the spring of 1917, the Albatros D-III, which could reach a speed of 109 mph. Nor were they well armed by contemporary standards, carrying only one .303-inch Lewis gun, with a 97-round ammunition drum (normally loaded with a few less, so as not to overstress the magazine spring) mounted on a quadrant device above the upper wing. That enabled the pilot to pull the butt of the gun down, setting it in a vertical position, to change drums (he usually carried two spares) or perhaps clear stoppages. "... [I]t was a frightening experience to be attacked or involved in a fight with one's gun down," recalled Willie Fry, remembering what it was like to try and dodge enemy fire while endeavouring to change a drum. "Many is the time I have thrown a full drum overboard and pushed the gun back into position with no drum. If I hadn't done so, I should not be alive to tell the tale."[13]

Even when it was lowered, the gun had to be set at an upward angle — about ten degrees — to ensure that the bullets issuing from its barrel would clear the tips of the propeller blades. In other words, there was a divergence between the direction of the aircraft's flight and the direction in which its gun fired.

> This was useful when attacking enemy machines from slightly behind and underneath … but it meant that in a diving attack … one had to dive this rather fragile machine steeply to get the sight on the target.
>
> … [I]f a satisfactory interrupter gear could have been found for a [belt-fed] Vickers gun to fire straight along the line of flight, through the propeller, for which the machine had been designed, it would have been an even more successful fighter. There was even a fitting for a Vickers gun built into all Nieuports.[14]

The optical (but not telescopic) tubular Aldis sight, mounted on the cockpit coaming, was angled even more sharply upward, so that the line of aim met the line of fire at a preset distance chosen by the pilot — usually somewhere between seventy and ninety yards. Thus one oddly tilted gun that needed to have its magazine changed after firing less than a hundred rounds was a distinct disadvantage in combat with the contemporary Albatros D-III, which boasted two belt-fed Spandaus — each belt normally carrying 250 rounds, "although more could be accommodated"[15] — synchronized to fire through the propeller arc, so that the line of sight and line of fire coincided.

The diminutive Nieuport could climb and turn better than any of its opponents, but unless taken entirely by surprise a German pilot could always open his throttle and dive away, since the Nieuport lacked both the power and the structural strength to keep up. Writing the squadron history at the end of the war, Jack Scott recalled that "some of these new machines ... began — to add to our troubles — to break up in the air."

> Caffyn's and Brackenbury's wings collapsed when firing at ground targets on the aerodrome, and the former was killed; while Ross's wings folded upwards when pulling out of a dive after firing a burst; he was badly injured, but has since recovered.... The reason for these accidents was that badly seasoned wood was being used by the French manufacturers, who also allowed a lot of little screws to be inserted in the main spars, thus weakening them considerably. HQ were informed and the matter was put right.[16]

As might be expected, given the nature of French bureaucracy, the matter was not put right quite that quickly, however. On 2 May, one pilot reported that his right lower wing had broken loose while in flight. His machine went into a spin when the wing broke, but since the lower wing was relatively small and provided little lift, it was possible for a skilful pilot to recover control and limp back to base. Scott noted at the time that "[t]his is the fourth Nieuport Scout to break in the air in 35 days. Luckily, Lieut. Fry is a good and fearless pilot."

However, the "troubles" that Scott cited in his interjection were not those of structural failure. He was referring to the losses that would lead British airmen to remember April 1917 as "bloody April." Nearly a year earlier, in the summer of 1916, the Germans had begun to group their single-seaters, formerly distributed at random among the multi-tasked *Flieger Abteilungen*, into dedicated units which they called *Jagdstaffeln* [fighter squadrons], or *Jastas* for short. Until that time there had been no specialization of function within squadrons; versatility had been the watchword. An airman, even one flying a single-seat fighter, might begin his day by strafing supply wagons or carrying out a tactical reconnaissance and end it by escorting bombers. He might be called upon to pilot a two-seater engaged in artillery observation work or tactical bombing of ground troops. Consequently, no real expertise had been developed in any aspect of operations. Now, however, pilots assigned to the *Jastas* began to concentrate on a specific facet of aerial warfare — that of destroying enemy aircraft in the air — and they quickly became rather better at it than their opponents, who were still generalists.

Jastas had an establishment of fourteen aircraft, compared with the eighteen of an RFC squadron. Seven of them had been formed by the end of August 1916, the first under the command of a thoughtful, innovative tactician, *Hauptmann* Oswald Boelcke. By the end of the year there were thirty-three *Jastas*,[17] while the RFC — slower off the mark, as it so often was, but recognizing the inevitable — could muster only eighteen fighter squadrons to oppose them.[18] *Jastas* were divided into two *Ketten*, while squadrons consisted of three flights. In the spring of 1917, these were the standard tactical elements, and lone wolves were becoming rare birds, to mix a metaphor.

The British had been slower still in recognizing Boelcke's new tactics, which essentially involved the leader focusing on one enemy machine, preferably an isolated one or a "tail-end Charlie," and attacking it while the remainder of his formation kept any other hostile aircraft in the vicinity busy ensuring their own survival. Then, it was on to the next victim. The technique proved highly successful and did much to enable German aces like von Richthofen (who took command of *Jasta* 11 on 14 January 1917) to accumulate so many victories.

Boelcke had been killed in October 1916 in a crash that followed a midair collision with one of his own men, but by the spring of 1917 his ideas were well established. Although they had only half the number of aircraft of the British and French, the Germans were inflicting inordinately high casualties on the RFC with their selective strategy and their technologically superior fighters.

Nevertheless, Trenchard continued to insist that his airmen maintain an offensive stance, pushing deep into German airspace at all places and times. This was particularly true when a major ground offensive was scheduled. The Battle of Arras, in which the Canadian Corps would take Vimy Ridge, giving the Entente its first unquestionable victory of the war, opened on 9 April 1917. The supporting air offensive had begun five days earlier, "so as to ensure the greatest measure of freedom to the corps aeroplanes," whose business it was, now that specialization was the rule, to direct and appraise artillery fire, monitor progress on the ground and support the advancing infantry by bombing and strafing the enemy.

> The total strength of the Royal Flying Corps along the whole front of the First and Third Armies was, for the opening of the Battle of Arras, twenty-five squadrons, representing 365 serviceable aeroplanes of which a third were single-seater fighters. Opposed to these two British armies was the German Sixth Army with an air strength of ... 195 aeroplanes, nearly one half of which were equipped for fighting.[19]

But what the Germans lacked in quantity they more than made up in quality as far as their fighter arm was concerned.

> On the five days from the 4th to the 8th of April, seventy-five British aeroplanes fell in action with a loss in flying personnel of 105.... In addition, there was an abnormally high number of flying accidents in

which, in the same brief period, fifty-six aeroplanes were wrecked and struck off the strength of the squadrons. These heavy losses by accidents were due in part to insufficiency of training which had been speeded up to danger point, and in part also to the strain imposed on pilots who had to meet in the air an enemy equipped, with few exceptions, with superior fighting aeroplanes.[20]

War Office calculations for the replacement of pilots in 1917 were based on a 230 percent per annum casualty rate, but in April 1917 the rate rose to 600 percent, which translated to an average of only two month's effective service from each pilot.[21] In the fighter squadrons, six weeks was about the average before a pilot was killed, wounded, taken prisoner or invalided home with "neurasthenia." Into this inhospitable environment, wearing a hugely expensive "glorious flying coat with fur collar and fur lining" given to him by Lady St. Helier,[22] plunged the brash young man from Owen Sound, anxious to make a name for himself. He had one great advantage besides that magnificent coat: seventy hours of air time in his logbook, as compared with the seventeen and a half hours logged by the average pilot joining a squadron in France.

Bishop, initially assigned to B Flight, made his first flight over the lines as "tail-end-Charlie" of a defensive patrol, on St. Patrick's Day. He found it a humbling experience. Anti-Zeppelin patrols had been flown as individuals and he had little or no appreciation of formation flying, but now it was suddenly important. As the junior pilot, he was assigned the most dangerous position. It was, of course, a foolish custom. If the flight was (rightly) to be led by its most experienced man, common sense should have suggested that the next most experienced man bring up the rear, where the danger of being surprised from behind was greatest. But, naturally, seniority had its privileges and newcomers were expendable.

There was also an undue emphasis placed upon maintaining a really tight formation, so that, except for the leader, the pilots involved had to spend nearly as much time watching their nearest neighbours and guarding against a collision as they did scanning the sky for hostile machines. Strangely, these fatuous rules remained RAF doctrine well into the Second World War when, learning from German practice, the "Vic" was finally dropped in favour of the much looser and tactically superior "finger four" grouping.[23]

Trailing the others, Bishop found it extraordinarily difficult to hold his place. Every time the formation turned "or did anything unexpected," he fell out of position and it took him what seemed like several minutes to get back. "But I got back every time as fast as I could. I felt safe when I was in the formation and scared when I was out of it."[24] The patrol split in two, three of them getting involved in driving off a German artillery observation machine. Bishop, having lost sight of his remaining comrades, was more concerned with finding them again. When he did so, he hung on their tails until all three landed safely after an hour's flight.[25] It was probably a typical fighter pilot's introduction to the Western Front.

His first success came only eight days later. During the late afternoon, he was one of four pilots patrolling at a height of some 9,000 feet in the vicinity of Arras. When three Albatroses began to stalk them, the flight commander allowed them to approach from behind until they were only just out of range. Then he turned his flight to meet the enemy and Bishop found a chance to strike.

One separating from the rest, lost height & attempted to come up behind our 2nd to the rear machine.
I dived and fired about 12 to 15 rounds. Tracers
went all around his machine. He dived steeply for
about 600 ft. and flattened out. I followed him and
opened fire from 40 to 50 yds. range, firing 40 to 50
rounds. A group of tracers went into the centre section, one being seen entering immediately behind
the pilot's seat and one seemed to hit himself. The
machine then fell out of control in a spinning nose
dive. I dived after him firing. When I reached 1500
or 2000 feet, my engine had oiled up and I glided
just over the [British] line. The Albatross [sic] Scout
when last seen by me was going vertically downwards at a height of 500 to 600 ft evidently out of
control and appeared to crash at _____. [Left blank
in original]

Why could he not specify where his victim fell? He provides his
not-unreasonable answer in *Winged Warfare*:

I have not to this day fully analysed my feelings in
those moments of my first victory. I don't think I fully
realized what it all meant. When I pulled my
machine out of its own somewhat dangerous dive, I
suddenly became conscious of the fact that I had not
the slightest idea in the world where I was. I had lost
all sense of direction and distance; nothing mattered
to me except the shooting down of that enemy scout
with the big black crosses that I shall never forget.[26]

His claim was confirmed by British antiaircraft gun crews who had watched the stricken machine hit the ground between Arras and the village of St. Leger. It was a spectacular beginning to what would be a spectacular career. "When I arrived back here I found myself a young hero," he told his father, in a letter written four days later. "I am now the only person in Number 60 who has brought down a Hun without help from other machines."[27] Trenchard sent a signal congratulating him, and Higgins and Pretyman appeared in person to offer their felicitations. "It appears that the great thing I did was the death dive of 7,000 ft with my engine full on," he told Margaret. "It has never been done before on a Nieuport, and they didn't think it would stand the strain. I'm glad I didn't know that, you may be sure."[28]

His triumph demonstrated the four qualities that made Bishop a superior fighter pilot: superb vision and an ability to constantly shift focus, no doubt enhanced by his earlier experience as an observer, that usually enabled him to see an opponent before the opponent saw him; what is now called situational awareness, or the ability to keep in mind the relative positions of every aircraft in the vicinity and work out mentally where they were likely to be in a few moments' time;[29] accurate shooting; and, not least, a willingness to push his aircraft past its nominal limits without worrying too much about the consequences. That last attribute proved fatal for many pilots, but Bishop was always lucky.

On 20 March, he was transferred to C Flight and switched to "a glorious machine, having an exceptionally good engine which is running beautifully at present." Scott had been vastly impressed by that first victory, and was determined to foster a budding talent; C Flight's commander, Captain Keith Caldwell, had just gone on leave, and Bishop was anointed an acting flight commander during his absence.

His first patrol as a leader was uneventful, but the second was something of a disaster. On 30 March, he was in charge of six machines when he saw a lone enemy aircraft half a mile below him. He dived on the German, his patrol in hot pursuit, only to find that they had been ambushed by five Albatroses — five in his combat report, made that day; *ten* in his book, written nine months later — lurking higher up. In a prolonged combat that carried them all far beyond the German lines, and during which Bishop escaped a combined attack by three of the enemy (his machine being badly damaged), two of his followers were shot down, one pilot being killed outright and the other mortally wounded.

The next day he registered a second witnessed victory while leading a patrol. Once again, "the 'Archie People' (antiaircraft) confirmed it all in their report, so he counts as my second Hun machine. The General and the Colonel both congratulated me this afternoon, so I take it that it means at least being 'mentioned in despatches.'" Apparently his ambitions were still quite moderate.

His second victory was followed by something of a lull over the next week — a week during which, for the first time, Bishop records having gone off on his own, "looking for a prize," on 2 April. By this stage of the war, solitary excursions were generally discouraged as being far too dangerous, but Scott, anxious to build his squadron's reputation, was prepared to extend special privileges to a promising novice who was anxious to fly as often as four times a day. The RFC's newly revised canon on air fighting, circulated only two weeks earlier, proclaimed that "as a principle single-seaters should not act alone," but accepted that "selected pilots on the fastest types of single-seaters may be usefully employed on a roving commission which will enable them to make the greatest use of surprise tactics."[30] However, the Nieuport was not the fastest type of single-seater in RFC service — the SE 5, now entering service, had a 10 mph edge. Nor did the staff attempt to define how pilots were to be chosen. Most commanding officers, living closer to reality than the staff types who conceived and promulgated doctrine, forbade all solitary excursions, and only the redoubtable Albert Ball (also flying a Nieuport) was being encouraged to fly alone.

But Scott was as much a "goer" in command as he had once been in the hunting field and was keen to build his squadron's reputation as an elite unit. Quite fearless himself, he was willing, even anxious, to encourage a promising novice avid to make a name for himself, and Bishop took every advantage of Scott's carte blanche. He would lead a dawn patrol, follow it with an individual sortie, take out a second patrol, and then go out again by himself in the evening. Most pilots were content, even proud, if they averaged two sorties a day.

"I picked a fight with the two-seaters whenever I could find one," he wrote, "and I searched for them high and low,"[31] although many experienced airmen thought that, when well handled, they were more dangerous opponents than single-seaters.[32] These particular adversaries, going about their business of artillery observation or reconnaissance, would usually work very close to, or immediately over, their front line. If one of them should be shot down it was almost certain to be seen falling by vigilant antiaircraft gunners, "balloonatics" — observers stationed in captive balloons just behind the lines — or perhaps the crew of an RFC two-seater engaged in similar duties. However, most of his recorded combats continued to be against single-seaters, and many of his later claims would made after flying alone, deep in enemy airspace, where there was virtually no possibility of either confirmation or refutation.

Some flights were entirely uneventful, others were not. He reported an indecisive fight with an Albatros, while flying alone again, on 6 April. That evening he led a six-plane patrol, "saw 6

H[ostile] A[ircraft] and followed them up and down in front of Vitry for 3/4 of an hour trying to engage them.... They seemed determined not to fight."[33]

On the 7th, he was one of four pilots ordered to attack kite balloons, a particularly dangerous task since they were always well protected by batteries of ground-based machine guns and often chaperoned by one or two fighters lurking in a nearby cloud. Pressing home an attack usually resulted in a Military Cross for those who succeeded, and all too often a wooden cross for those who failed. It was one or the other, since MCs were not granted posthumously — for some bizarre reason, only VCs and Mentions in Despatches (MiDs) were in the posthumous award category.

> Although incendiary bullets were used, the hydrogen [filled] bag was quite difficult to ignite because the hydrogen first had to combine with the oxygen in the air to form a combustible mixture and ... the gas was concentrated in the upper portion of the envelope. It was impossible to dive on the balloon from above because when the explosion occurred the immense sheets of flame surged skyward and the attacker, diving into it, was guaranteed sure death; therefore, the balloon had to be approached from the side. The most successful method used in attacking these inflammable giants was to approach the target at high speed, flying at tree-top level, or lower. At about one hundred yards the attacking plane usually began firing at the upper half of the bag in order to allow the gas to escape and continued to fire steadily at the one point until, at about fifty yards,

the bag usually burst into flame and the attacker
then turned sharply in order to escape injury.[34]

In this case, although there were no flames, only one pilot was
considered to have succeeded — and he was credited with an enemy
fighter as well. Bishop's combat report recounted what happened:

> While diving at a hostile balloon an Albatros Scout
> engaged me from behind. I turned and fired 15 to
> 20 rounds at 100 yds. range. Tracers were seen going
> into his machine, he dived away steeply. I dived on
> the balloon, which was then on the ground, and
> opened fire at 800 ft., finishing my drum when
> approximately 50 ft. above it. Nearly all of the bul-
> lets entered the balloon and black smoke was visible
> coming out of it in 2 places.[35]

Since he had been on a specific assignment to attack this balloon, his magazine had probably been filled with the new
Buckingham incendiary ammunition, expressly designed to set
balloons afire. Such a bullet, entering the top of the gasbag of a
balloon in the air, would certainly cause the balloon to explode in
flame; but one in the lower part of the bag of a largely deflated balloon on or near the ground would most probably only cause the
fabric to smoulder around the edge of the hole, causing the "black
smoke" that Bishop noted. However, Scott promptly credited him
with destroying both the balloon and the Albatros, even though
Bishop had only reported the latter as having "dived away steeply."

He was quick to take up Scott's lead, and a letter to Margaret,
written that same day, struck a more decisive note than the combat
report had done. Now there was flame.

I saw my balloon under me when I was only 6,000
ft up, so I dived on it. At the same time a Hun
dived on me and filled my machine with holes. I
turned on him and in a short scrap shot him
down. In the meantime, the Huns had pulled the
balloon down to the ground, so down I went after
it, to a height of 50 feet, and set it on fire.... I
think I am fairly certain of getting a decoration for
it. Tonight the general-commanding RFC
[Trenchard] wired my CO [Scott], "Congratulate
Lieut. Bishop on his fine feat today," so I am very
bucked with life tonight.

In the early evening, perhaps while Bishop was writing his letter, Manfred von Richthofen and four of his pilots flying Albatros D-
IIIs met a six-plane flight of 60 Squadron and "made short work of
three of the single-gun, less manoeuvrable Nieuports."[36] This may
have been the closest Bishop ever got to actually tangling with the
Red Baron, despite a story he would subsequently invent about a
fight on the last day of the month.

Maurice Baring, Trenchard's military secretary, recorded in
his diary that he and his master arrived at Filescamp Farm the next
day (in the course of visiting eleven squadrons on half a dozen airfields) and "talked to all the pilots."[37] After losing three pilots just
the day before, 60 Squadron, for one, probably needed some
cheering up. No doubt Trenchard also offered his personal congratulations to Bishop, supplementing his signal of the previous
evening, but Bishop makes no mention of the visit. Nor does he
refer to the arrival of Albert Ball, the RFC's current "top gun,"
while Trenchard was on the premises, so to speak. Ball, newly
posted to 56 Squadron, was chasing Trenchard, seeking permis-

sion to swap an SE 5, with which Number 56 was equipped, for his old favourite, a Nieuport 17.*

Instead, two of Bishop's letters have Trenchard visiting two days later, on the 10th (when, according to Baring, the GOC was at his headquarters all day), and even then he makes no mention of Ball's appearance. It has been asserted that the idea for a dawn strafe of a German airfield originated with Ball, and that he sounded out Bishop with the idea of them doing it together. There is no hard evidence of that (and, as we shall see, in *Winged Warfare* Bishop was going to claim that he thought the thing through himself), but what are we to make of his note to Margaret on 18 April that "Ball ... is coming over to see me, I believe tonight." That certainly sounds as if Ball wanted to talk business, although Bishop's next letter, on the 21st, makes no mention of the visit, or of any arrangement the two men may have come to.

In the spring of 1917, finding and keeping a British aerial paladin was proving a frustrating business. Major Lionel Rees, MC, had been credited with eight victories when he was seriously wounded while winning a VC in July 1916, and never flew operationally again. Lieutenant Patrick Langan-Byrne, DSO, after destroying ten enemy machines, had been killed by Boelcke in October, and Major Lanoe Hawker, VC, with seven victories to his credit, fell victim to von Richthofen in November. In that same month another Canadian, Captain Alan Bell-Irving, had also accounted for seven when he was wounded so seriously that he was never able to fly operationally again. Captain Sidney Cowan, MC and two Bars, had seven victories to his credit when he was killed in a collision

---

* He would soon come to realize that the SE 5 was the better machine, and he would be flying one when he was killed, a month later.

with another British aircraft a week after Bell-Irving's wounding. Captain Arthur Knight, DSO, MC, had also tallied seven victories when he was badly wounded by the Red Baron in December, and he, like Bell-Irving, never flew operationally again. A number of others who had shown promise had succumbed to combat fatigue and been posted home for rest and recuperation. Some returned to the front in 1918, but others never did, taking up administrative or training appointments.

Meanwhile, the danger of a mass breakdown in RFC morale had clearly become a possibility, if not a likelihood, and the preservation of morale required that successful individuals be singled out for special attention. Propaganda was becoming just as important as performance. The willingness of everyone in the chain of command to push the facts related in Bishop's combat reports to a favourable but unwarranted conclusion suggests how anxious the authorities were to build role models for its airmen at a time when the enemy was dominant in the air and Imperial champions thin on the ground. Twenty-year-old Albert Ball, credited with thirty-one victories during his first tour at the front, was the designated British contender for the moment, but who could say how long he would last, now that he was back in action? There was always room for another likely lad, and this young Bishop showed promise.

Thus Jack Scott, ambitious for his pilots if not for himself, chose to take his protégé's word for what happened on those increasingly frequent individual sorties and, as we have seen, even embellished his reports on occasion, his embroidery perhaps made easier by Bishop's personality, which seems to have charmed almost everyone who did not know him well — and many of those who did.

> It was curious to notice how quick the mechanics of
> the squadron were to recognise Bishop's quality.

Only a few days after his arrival at the squadron the sergeants gave a musical evening to which the officers were invited, and it was observed that one of the very few toasts which were proposed by them was that of Bishop's health, although at this time he had only destroyed one enemy machine and none of his fellow-officers had, as yet, any idea of the brilliant career that was in store for him.[38]

He may have charmed Scott and the other ranks on the squadron, but not everyone felt that comfortable with him. When Willie Fry left Filescamp at the end of June, after two months as deputy flight commander, "[a]lthough I had lived and flown with Bishop as my flight commander during the previous two months I had never really got to know him or make friends with him.... He was very popular in the squadron, yet I do not remember him having any particular friends."[39]

It may be argued that Fry's judgment was skewed by the fact that he eventually left 60 Squadron over his refusal to apologize for "a remark I had made to my flight commander." Scott took Bishop's side, giving Fry the choice of either apologizing or being posted to the Home Establishment, and Fry chose to go home.* But his judgment on Bishop is endorsed by Sholto Douglas who, in his memoir, observes that "I knew Bishop fairly well, and from time to time I came to see quite a lot of him; but there was something about him that left one feeling that he preferred to live as he fought, in a rather brittle, hard world of his own."[40] *Winged Warfare* simply reinforces those opinions: every other First World War airman's memoir names some of his

---

* Fry does not tell us what the offending remark was, but Phil Markham, who spoke with him in 1978, said that he intimated it related to the VC award. Might Fry have questioned whether it was truly earned?

companions in peril, but Bishop's story focuses totally on himself. No mention by name of such loyal comrades as Fry, Keith (Grid) Caldwell, or Spencer (Nigger) Horn, with whom he flew many a dawn patrol. Even Jack Scott, to whom he owed so much, earns only perfunctory mentions as "the Major" or "my Major."

On 8 April, as the Third Army braced for the Battle of Arras and the Canadian Corps made final preparations to storm up Vimy Ridge, Bishop's calibre was confirmed in Scott's eyes when the latter personally led a five-machine patrol that included the Canadian. They encountered "a large pack of Huns" chasing after "a small patrol of Sopwith two-seaters,"[41] and the fire-eating Scott happily charged into the enemy formation. Bishop drove a two-seater off his leader's tail, which "flew away eastwards after I had fired 40 rounds at him, tracers hit his machine in fuselage & planes."

> I then dived at a balloon from 5,000 feet and drove it down to the ground. It did not smoke. I climbed to 4,000 [ft] and engaged an Albatross [sic] Scout, fired the remainder of my drum at him, dodged away and put a new drum on, and engaged him again. After two bursts he dived vertically and was still in a nose dive when about 500 feet from the ground. I then climbed to 10,000 [ft] and 5 miles NE of Arras I engaged 2 Single Seaters flying towards our lines. 3 more machines were above and behind. I fired the remainder of my drum into the pair, one burst of 15 at one and the rest at the second one. The former turned and flew away with his nose well down, the 2nd one went down in a spinning nose dive, my tracers hit all

around the pilot's seat and I think he must have been hit. Then I climbed and got behind the other three about the vicinity of Vitry. I engaged them and one, a double seater, went down in a nose dive but I think partly under control. Then I engaged the remaining 2 and finished my third drum at them. They both flew away eastward.[42]

Although neither of his possible victims were seen to hit the ground, Scott (who may have seen them fall himself) confirmed both of them, together with one by Lieutenant W.E. Molesworth, another member of the patrol. That put Bishop's score up to five, making him an ace by Entente standards, and "then the CO gave me his touring car and I spent yesterday going around and seeing my friends, also today."[43]

CHAPTER 3

Tricks of the Trade

The weather had turned bad and there was little or no flying for the next week. On 18 April 1917, Bishop wrote to Margaret that "I feel absolutely played out from flying too much and this spell of dud weather has been a Godsend, absolutely." He had been flying, mostly in hostile airspace, for four or five hours a day — at least half of the time alone — and one can only wonder at the combination of ambition that drove him on and psychological fortitude that enabled him to bear the stress. "Bloody April" was taking its toll: in the four-week period ending 27 April, RFC/RNAS casualties amounted to 238 killed or missing and 105 wounded, compared with German losses of 49 killed or missing and 19 wounded.[1] Every day, in every squadron on the Western Front, brave men who averaged less than half as much flying per day as Bishop — and that in company — were noting their lost comrades and slowly losing their nerve until, if they were lucky, they were posted home, emotional wrecks.

Bishop claimed his next victory, his eighth, on 20 April, when Scott, for whatever reason, chose to annotate his combat report to the effect that "Lieut. Bishop went out by himself on this occasion."

Of course, he had begun to do that two weeks earlier and was now doing so frequently.

> I engaged a two-seater by getting under him and firing with my gun pulled down [i.e., with the butt pulled down on the Foster mounting, as if he was about to change ammunition drums] at a range of 10 to 20 yds. I fired about 10 to 15 rounds, then dived twice, firing from 100 yds range. I dived a third time, opening fire at 30 yds range, and looking back after passing saw smoke was coming out around the pilot's seat. In a few seconds flames were visible and the machine fell in a volume of smoke. I fired 80 rounds in all.[2]

His claim, confirmed and passed along by Scott, was promptly recorded as a victory in both the brigade summary and the RFC communiqué, but it seems that only one German airman fell that day: the pilot of a *Jasta 10* single-seater, wounded in action far from the scene of Bishop's alleged victory.[3] Bishop reported that the engagement took place in the vicinity of Biache St. Vaast — just west of Vitry-en-Artois and some ten or twelve miles beyond the German front line, where there was no prospect of it being reported by any friendly agency, either in the air or on the ground. If he was really that far behind the German lines in an aircraft that, although nimble, was not as fast as any of the enemy's first-line fighters, it could be argued that he was deserving of a decoration just for being there.

With heavy losses among the two-seater corps machines that were normally responsible for tactical photo-reconnaissance, even when escorted by fighters, some staff officer had the bright idea of fitting cameras in single-seaters for such missions as were within their range. A camera-equipped Nieuport scout, escorted by other Nieuports, would have a distinctly better chance of succeeding and surviving than a slower, less manoeuvrable, corps machine.

> The camera was fitted in a slung rubber-suspended frame inside the fuselage behind the pilot's seat with a hole cut in the bottom fabric under the lens. We had to fly as level as we could judge and manage when exposing plates, and were given the height — to which the lens had been set — at which to fly while taking photos. This was not very high; as far as I recall, it was between 8,000 and 10,000 feet. The camera control for exposing plates was manipulated by means of a Bowden cable to the cockpit with a release and re-tension gadget. We were told to fly over the target area at a set air-speed and to make exposures at a given interval of seconds.[4]

When 60 Squadron was designated to take photographs of an area some seven miles beyond the enemy front line using this new equipment and technique, it was typical of Scott that he decided to carry out the first such venture himself. He attempted to do so "near Vis-en-Artois," and was promptly attacked by several German scouts. Bishop, however, was lurking a little higher up with a covering patrol and awaiting his chance.

> … I dived to the assistance of Major Scott, 2,000 ft below me. He was attacked by 5 single-seaters. I fired 15 rounds at one and he dived steeply, apparently damaged. I then attacked a second one from the flank and fired 20 rounds at him, most of the bullets

apparently hitting his machine. He went down through the clouds apparently out of control.[5]

Scott added a rider to this combat report, to the effect that "The remainder of the O[ffensive] P[atrol] dived but were too late to catch the H[ostile] A[ircraft] who all went down vertically through the clouds." Bishop was not credited with the machine that "dived steeply, apparently damaged," but the one that "went down through the clouds apparently out of control" became his ninth victory. Scott knew very well, however, that the evidence was far from convincing. In his post-war *History of 60 Squadron*, he would note that "sometimes this [technique] was used as a 'blind' by some pilots to escape. They simply let the machine do what it liked, and when near the ground took control again."[6] In fact, just that approach was advocated in the RFC memorandum *Fighting in the Air* of March 1917: "If surprised in an unfavourable position … the best chance [of escape] lies in a side-slip, or a fall [apparently] out of control."[7]

British airmen and RFC morale were both waning as fast as Bishop's star was waxing. One undistinguished participant serving in another squadron at this time has recorded how, during the spring of the year:

> Our casualties mounted alarmingly. There was hardly an evening when the same people gathered in the mess. It was here that a certain amount of frank and free comment on our casualty rate could be heard … our commanding officer discouraged it; but it continued.…
>
> This feeling, although officially looked on as defeatist, was prevalent among operational pilots.…

Officers of the higher command, from Major
General Hugh Trenchard, as he was then, down to
the commanders of wings, according to the critics
were throwing away aircraft and lives for no dis-
cernible purpose. At any rate, they did not convince
their pilots that there was a purpose.[8]

Scott's squadron was one of those that suffered most heavily but,
perhaps because of his leadership, it had less of a morale problem
than most. "From the last week in March to the last week in May
our losses were very severe," he wrote. "In fact, counting those who
went sick and those injured in crashes on our side of the line, we
lost thirty-five officers during these eight weeks, almost twice the
strength of the squadron."[9]

Short of Trenchard changing his strategy from an unbridled
offensive to a selective one until such time as his airmen could be
equipped with better machines, there seemed only one way to
strengthen RFC morale. That was to create British champions
whose deeds would match or surpass those of von Richthofen and
his ilk, heroes who could serve as role models for the torrent of inex-
perienced replacement pilots pouring into France. The home front,
faced with the appalling casualty rates of attrition warfare on the
ground and weakened by industrial strikes (not to mention the
growing menace of Gotha bombers, which had now replaced
Zeppelins in bombing London and east coast population centres),
also needed a morale boost. Reports in *The Times* that "the Prince
of Wales has returned to the front" and "the King is now slicing his
own bread," or a glowing biography of yet another fierce-looking but
inept general, were no longer enough. Public relations — or propaganda — was not, however, a generally accepted aspect of the
Imperial way of war, and it was still not British policy to advertise

individuals unless they held high rank or had attained the ultimate recognition of valour with the award of a Victoria Cross.

Young Albert Ball from Nottinghshire did not have a VC as yet, although his feats were becoming widely celebrated within the flying services.

> By the beginning of May the name that Albert Ball had made for himself was something to conjure with. In the short space of only just over a year this modest and gentle young man — he was still only twenty years of age when he was killed — became a legend in the RFC for his displays of sheer audacity. He was probably the most aggressive fighter pilot that the Air Force has ever had, and there can be little doubt that he must have gladdened enormously the heart of "Boom" Trenchard.* Flying with extraordinary daring, Ball would tackle, single-handed, any size of enemy formation, hurling himself at them and throwing them into confusion.[10]

The local Nottingham papers had no doubt emphasized the citations for his MC and two DSOs, as published in the *London Gazette*, but that was certainly the only way in which his name would have come to civilian attention. In May 1917, *The Times* could print a quarter-column under the headline "British Airmen's Great Fight" without mentioning any of them by name, while at the same time not hesitating to inform its readers that the French aces Guynemer and Nungesser had now accounted for thirty-eight and twenty-four German machines respectively. Even the Germans got their due, with

---

* Trenchard's booming bass voice was responsible for his nickname.

extracts from their latest communiqué. "Lieutenant Wolff shot down his 28th and 29th opponents and Lieutenant Schaefer his 24th and 25th."[11] Regrettably, however, a stiff upper lip and firm restraint was still the British way of warfare.

Bishop went out twice more in the afternoon of the 22nd, reporting that he had attacked four Albatros scouts but that in each case they had escaped — or, as he told his mother, "I had four more scraps but no luck at all."[12] In the evening, he flew two more sorties as leader of patrols which encountered no enemy aircraft. This was the first time he flew *five* sorties in a single day — three in company and two alone.

On the 23rd he managed four solo sorties and one leading a patrol, but his two claims, one destroyed and one DDOOC, both came on his third flight, while he was alone. First, he said, he found a German two-seater, and "after a short burst he seemed to be hit and dived."

> I dived after him firing all the way. He landed in a field near Vitry and I finished the rest of my drum at him on the ground. So far as I could see neither pilot nor observer got out of the machine.
>
> At 3.59 pm, at 6,000 ft [Map] Sheet 51 near I 7, I went to the assistance of another Nieuport attacked by three Albatross [sic] Scouts. I attacked from behind on the same level and took one of them by surprise. He fell out of control and as one of the other H.A. was diving steeply and the other one flying away pursued by the Nieuport, I followed him down and saw him crash at [map reference] I. 2.[13]

Who, one wonders, was flying this other Nieuport, alone and well over the German side of the lines in the vicinity of Vitry? It should have been easy to find out — there were only three other British squadrons flying Nieuports on the Western Front, and one of them was also based at Filescamp, but there seems to have been no pilot in either of those squadrons reckless enough to fly alone in such a dangerous spot. Could it have been Albert Ball, now back in Flanders and flying his specially assigned Nieuport out of Vert Galand, some twenty-five miles south of Le Hameau? Whoever it was (if it was not another product of Bishop's imagination), no one came forward to back up his claim.

In the evening he was out again and, seeing a fight going on in the distance over Croisille, "I flew in that direction." He fired some twenty rounds at one adversary about 200 yards away, "as we passed, but after turning I could not find him again." This time there were other airmen in the vicinity, including Scott, who noted on Bishop's combat report that "as a spectator I saw two H.A. go down between Guemappe and Vis-en-Artois, but a good many aircraft were involved in this mêlée, any one of which might have done the damage."[14] Oddly enough, Bishop made no claim.

On the 27th, he was credited with another kite balloon after he attacked one in the air "about 4 miles west of Vitry" and "saw the balloon smoking. I then fired about 10 rounds into the basket as I had seen no one jump out."[15] Again Scott credited him with a balloon destroyed, although there was no hard claim from Bishop and no supporting evidence. However, the smoking balloon had become a flaming balloon when he wrote to Margaret about it. "I shot down another balloon in flames and I think I killed the two people in the basket. It was great fun," he reported jubilantly. "By the way, there are only eight people in the RFC who have over eight Huns, and I am one."[16] Nevertheless, "I began to feel that my list of

victims was not climbing as steadily as I would have liked," he recollected in *Winged Warfare*. Ball was constantly adding to his score
and "I felt I had to keep going if I was to be second to him."[17]

Two days later, promoted to captain, he was out alone once
again, this time at 17,000 feet, east of Epinoy. Height was vitally
important to all fighter pilots, especially to those flying alone in relatively slow machines, but in 1917 no British flyers enjoyed the ben-
efits of supplementary oxygen. Doctors attached to the RFC were
aware of many of the problems posed by hypoxia — including the
deterioration in visual acuity, a matter of particular importance to
pilots flying alone, as Bishop so often was — which were more
noticeable in cold weather than in warm, but the weight and com-
plexity of oxygen breathing equipment seems to have been considered a greater handicap than the lack of oxygen itself.

It was always cold up there (20 degrees Celsius at ground level
translated to minus-15 at 17,000 feet), but presumably Lady St. Helier's
well-chosen gift was serving its purpose and Bishop seems to have been
in his usual good form, his vision little affected by the height. He reported being well above four other Nieuports which were escorting some
FE two-seaters. Glimpsing an enemy fighter 3,000 feet below him but
still above the other British machines, he dived on it from out of the sun
and, after expending almost a whole drum of ammunition, claimed
that "at about 11,000 ft [his victim] burst into flames."[18] There were, by
his own account, four Nieuports and some FEs below him, and a
"flamer" with its trail of smoke should have been easy to see as it fell
past them. No one reported seeing it fall, however.

In the absence of complete German records, it is impossible to say
with certainty which of these uncorroborated claims were true, which
were the result of genuine misapprehension and which were fraudu-
lent. But there can be no doubt that, in *Winged Warfare*, Bishop mis-
led his readers about the events of 30 April. After recounting several

indecisive engagements during the morning (one of them against three-seater Gotha G-IV bombers, rare birds on the Western Front by day and yet never mentioned in his combat report), and another allegedly involving "five scarlet Albatross [sic] scouts," he wrote that he was in the company of Scott during the afternoon, when "we discovered four red Albatrosses just to our right. This latter quartette, I believe, was made up of Baron von Richthofen and three of his best men."[19]

His combat report, drafted immediately after landing and initialled by Scott, was the usual matter-of-fact account that made no mention of the colour of his opponents' machines, nor of von Richthofen.

> I attacked 4 H[ostile] A[ircraft] from behind and
> above. I fired 2 bursts of 5 rounds each at the
> leader who had turned, I then fired 10 rounds at
> the rear man with no apparent result. Seeing four
> more machines diving from above, I zoomed up &
> found they were [RNAS] triplanes. The four H.A.
> then disappeared.[20]

Scott's report was just as laconic. After listing the type of flight as "Recreation" (a euphemism commonly used by commanding officers who were not supposed to fly operationally but were bold enough to do so) he reported that he had:

> ... attacked 4 H.A. E[ast] of Lens. I fired bursts of 10
> shots at one machine which turned over on its back but
> recovered and dived. My gun had stopped No 3 stop-
> page due presumably to bad ammunition. When [I]
> recocked gun I heard machine gun fire and observed
> tracers passing to my left, one of which hit my machine.
> I engaged this H.A. and had all I could do to keep out

of his fire for some seconds. I then got my gun on to him, fired a burst of 20/25 [rounds] when H.A. put his nose down and dived vertically.[21]

No mention of the Red Baron, or of the colour of the enemy machines!

The letter that Bishop wrote to Margaret that evening was rather more dramatic, but there was still no mention of von Richthofen or red-painted enemies: "… the CO and I went out and got mixed up with four really good Huns. We chased them away, but oh heavens, did they shoot well. Seven bullets went through my machine within six inches of me, and one within an inch…"[22] A little more than half a year later, however, in *Winged Warfare*, von Richthofen's presence had become a hard fact.

I opened fire on the Baron, and in another half-moment found myself in the midst of what seemed to be a stampede of blood-thirsty animals. Everywhere I turned smoking bullets were jumping at me…. Once my gun jammed, and … I had to "fuss" with the weapon until I got it right again. I had just got going again when von Richthofen flashed by me and I let him have a short burst …[23]

The big flaw in all this is that we know Manfred von Richthofen did not fly at all on the last day of "Bloody April." His father had arrived at Roucourt, where *Jasta 11* was housed in a local chateau, on the 29th, just in time to applaud his elder son's fiftieth victory, and Manfred, forbidden to fly again until the Kaiser had personally congratulated him, spent the next day entertaining the old man and celebrating his half-century.[24] Younger brother Lothar, also with

Jasta 11, did fly several times on the 30th, claiming his fifteenth and sixteenth victims, but the descriptions of his fights do not match in any way the accounts of Bishop and Scott. Whomever they met, it was not either of the von Richthofen brothers.

Bishop's second kite balloon might easily have brought him a Bar to his MC, but Scott had much bigger things in mind. Earlier on the 30th, Bishop had been leading an offensive patrol [OP] over Lens, Monchy-le-Preux and Wancourt when he became involved in a series of fights and was credited with one machine destroyed, even though the last he saw of it was "in a spin and only about 1,000 ft from the ground."[25] Then, on 2 May, while returning from leading a patrol that had been escorting a photo-reconnaissance mission, but having left the patrol to find its own way back:

> I manoeuvred to catch one party of three [two-seaters] when just W[est] of the Quéant-Drocourt line, as that was the nearest they were coming to our lines.
>
> I attacked the rear one and after one burst of 15 rounds he fell out of control and crashed.... While [I was] watching him another two-seater came up under me and opened fire. I attacked him firing about 40 rounds. He fell out of control and I followed him about 1,500 ft, finishing my drum. He was in a spinning nose dive and my shots could be seen entering all around the pilot's and observer's seats. Three more HA being above me, I returned.[26]

Again there was no confirmation from any third party, but he was credited with two more "kills" by Scott, who felt that these successes justified a DSO. Or might it have originally been a citation for something more, downgraded to a DSO by someone in higher authority? In a 1 June 1917 letter to Margaret (the day before he would fly the sortie that brought him his VC), Bishop mentioned, "as the greatest secret," that "I have just learnt that when I got my DSO, I was recommended for the VC."[27]

Whatever the citation had originally proposed by way of reward, the DSO version published in the *London Gazette* recorded that he had "attacked three hostile machines, two of which he brought down, although in the meantime he was himself attacked by four hostile machines." That, of course, exaggerates the report that he had made. It seems that Scott would go to almost any length to glorify his protégé, but his underlying concern — and that of Pretyman, Higgins, et al. — was probably more for the morale of the RFC than the glorification of Bishop. The *Gazette* citation concluded by emphasizing the standard he was setting for his peers. "His courage and determination have set a fine example to others."[28] And examples of courage and determination were what the RFC desperately needed.

The way in which his reports were embellished by Scott (who would have scorned to do so with his own) cannot have been lost on Bishop, and only encouraged him to transform perfunctory or imaginary encounters into victorious combats. These may have been mental processes that occurred more frequently after Ball's now-imminent death, as Bishop became obsessed with retaining his status as the RFC's leading ace and building a score to rival that of von Richthofen.

MCs were hardly commonplace on the Western Front in 1917, but nor were they really rare. DSOs were, at least when worn by junior officers. There were three ways to earn one. The first was to be the commander of a battalion, squadron, brigade or division that had performed particularly well in battle; the second was to be a senior officer who had excelled in staff work or administration. The third was to distinguish oneself by great personal bravery, irrespective of rank, and be rewarded with what, in such a case, was often spoken of as "the poor man's VC."

There could be little doubt as to which category a stripling in his early twenties, with the relatively lowly rank of captain, belonged in. Bishop would now, in due course (his DSO would come on 9 May, although not gazetted until mid-June), enjoy the renown that he sought so eagerly everywhere he went. Meanwhile, the more recognition he received, the more he sought, driving himself to foolish extremes that leave one wondering how he could possibly have survived to fight another day. At 2 p.m. on 2 May, "I am dead tired already," he wrote to Margaret, before obsessing again about Albert Ball.

> I have done four hours flying already today and am now standing by for another show. This morning 11 of us went out, and I managed to get separated in a scrap which took place. During the return trip I was fighting all the time and to my intense joy got two big fat Huns down.... Ball is the only person in the RFC who has more down than I have.[29]

Later that same day, flying alone, he used up all his ammunition in four different fights, claiming one enemy "evidently having been forced to land."[30] For some unexplained reason, this claim was not granted. Nevertheless, Bishop's total now stood at sixteen (including two balloons), while Ball had added four in two days to raise his score to forty.

On 3 May, "while leading OP I dived on two E[nemy] A[ircraft]* doing Art[illery] Obs[ervation]. I fired [a] drum at each from long

---

* In the spring of 1917 the terminology was changing, from "Hostile Aircraft." Many airmen failed to remember the change when writing up their combat reports.

range. They flew away and did not return. The rest of the patrol was unable to get within range."[31] Several Nieuports would have been easier for the enemy to see in good time than one solitary machine, and a pair of two-seaters would have been wise to flee, but again he had been unsuccessful while in company, although he had got close enough to make it worthwhile opening fire. Much the same thing happened, with exactly the same result, during another offensive patrol that evening. When witnesses were to hand, Bishop was consistently less successful.

The next day he apparently shared a victory with his deputy flight commander, Willie Fry.

> With Lieut. Fry following me I dived at two two-seaters. I fired twenty rounds at one and turned off, Lieut. Fry diving on and firing. I dived again as he stopped firing and fired about forty rounds, in the course of which the observer stopped firing. The machine did two turns of a spin and then nose dived to earth where we saw him crash. I fired a short burst at long range at the second one which flew away and did not return.[32]

An addendum to this report — typewritten, and concluded with the words "(signed) Lieut. Fry," but no actual handwritten signature — records that "I dived with Capt. Bishop and fired a long burst at close range at the same time as him. The H.A. spun and crashed W of Brebières," while someone (presumably Scott, who had not been present) added a second note to the effect that "five scouts were 1,500 feet above Capt. Bishop and Lt. Fry, during all this time they did not come down."

In *Air of Battle*, Willie Fry quotes from his logbook: "[Nieuport] B.1597. 1hr. [flight.] 1 H[ostile] A[ircraft] brought down and crashed near Brebières with Bishop," and then observes that, "Strangely, although I must have flown with him constantly as his deputy leader in the flight during the next two months [and squadron records confirm that he did] this is the only mention in my logbook of being involved with Bishop in a fight."[33] Was Fry trying to tell the reader obliquely something that he did not want to say outright? Why "strangely"? What exactly was he implying? He offered a very different version of this incident in a letter written to Phil Markham nearly twenty years later, in 1994.

> One day (my logbook says 4 May 1917), soon after I had arrived back in the squadron, we were at luncheon in the mess when a message was brought in to the CO that a German two-seater was operating and taking photographs on the front of the right-hand corps of the 3rd Army on the Arras front, and would we drive it away or shoot it down. The CO asked Bishop and myself to go up after it and we were in the air within a few minutes. On getting up to the trench lines, we saw at once the German machine, straight in front and slightly higher than we were. I can see it now, after all these years, a black blob, and slightly above us. It turned away as we approached and we both let fly at it at long range, too far away to have any chance of hitting him.
>
> Having driven him off, we turned for home. On landing, Bishop came up to me and, to my surprise, said, "We got him all right. Did you see him go down and crash?" ' — or something like that. Now I had not seen a German machine go down. The machine which I had taken to be the one we were attacking,

and at which I had fired a burst at very long range, had turned back, deep into the German lines. But such was Bishop's reputation in the squadron that I thought he must have attacked and brought down another, closer, machine which I had not seen. I was certainly not going to contradict him. I was young [aged 21] and unsure of myself, feeling very much on trial under new management, and was not going to jeopardize my place in the squadron.

This was the occasion on which we did the job and went back and finished our luncheon.... Ever since, and over all the years, I have had that flight on my mind, and can still recollect the sight of the German two-seater turning sharply away and giving me the first suspicions as to my flight commander's credibility. But at the time it would not have entered my head to express any doubts. I did not make out a combat report, but Bishop, in his, gave me credit for doing so [sic] with him, so I shared the credit in Major Scott's report.[34]

Did they meet one enemy or two? And what actually happened to it — or them? Although his first victory, an Albatros D-III "driven down out of control," had been achieved only two days earlier, Fry was no novice. He had already completed one tour as a pilot on the Western Front, in 11, 12 and (briefly) 60 Squadrons, and normally no one would have questioned his ability to see, in an otherwise empty sky, whether he was involved with one or two opponents. Did he, personally, know about the typewritten annotation to Bishop's combat report, or did someone [Bishop?] simply draft a comment for him and type his name in? From what we already know of Bishop it would have been quite in line with his ambition, and his cavalier attitude towards the truth, to argue for a second enemy machine that was never there and attempt to buttress his claim with a piece of mild forgery. Whatever the case, by mid-July this particular kill, initially credited as a half-victory for Bishop, would have quietly and unobtrusively grown to be a whole!

On 7 May, Bishop flew three times, once leading his flight and twice by himself. Flying alone in the morning, he claimed to have dived on an Albatros from up-sun and "with the speed from my dive, I overtook him flying underneath. I pulled my gun down and opened fire from 15 yds range firing twenty rounds.... He fell in a spin and smoke was coming from the machine."[35] If he is to be believed, he fired from an unusually short range (getting close and then shooting straight seem to have been the common attributes of most aces), but once again there was no conclusive evidence as to what happened to his opponent. No witness. And even if events did unfold as Bishop claimed, the smoke could easily have been oil burning in an over-revving engine.

A curious factor in all these individual enterprises, however, is the number of occasions on which Bishop claimed to have shot down single-seaters that were also flying alone; or, if they were not alone, he makes no mention of their companions who could be expected to try and assist or avenge their hapless comrade. Two-seaters engaged in reconnaissance or artillery observation and content to flee at the first sign of trouble might operate unaccompanied (or with fighter cover that would fail to intervene in time), but only one man on the German side, *Leutnant* Werner Voss — perhaps the greatest air fighter of all — and Bishop and Ball in the British ranks, habitually flew alone any more. For most other fighter pilots, even the idea of going into combat alone was anathema. Their formations would inevitably be broken up, as the action developed, into one-on-one, but they would not be individually overwhelmed by sheer numbers and thus meet the fate of Voss, finally trapped and shot down in a Homeric fight with seven pilots of 56 Squadron (three of them already aces) on 23 September 1917.

Bishop's last fight of the day found him leading an escort to some two-seaters engaged in tactical bombing which were attacked by a formation of Albatroses. He claimed one of the enemy machines driven down "completely out of control" in his combat report, but that assessment was crossed out, presumably by Scott, who noted that "an observer in 11 Sqn saw H.A. land under control."[36] Nevertheless, the brigade summary for the day credited him with one enemy aircraft "in a spin, smoking," and a second "probably out of control." These became two "driven down, out of control" in RFC Communiqué Number87. Higgins and Trenchard were doing their bit to build the Bishop legend.

Meanwhile, Albert Ball was making his last flight. Ironically, it was not in the course of one of his trademark individual exploits; nor, apparently, was he shot down by some superior or lucky pilot. The exact circumstances of his death remain obscure, but on 7 May he was leading a formation of 56 Squadron on an evening patrol when it tangled with part of von Richthofen's *Jasta 11* (although the Red Baron himself was not present on this occasion, either). In the course of a muddled, chaotic fight through low cloud, Ball crashed and died. The Germans, never averse to building up Manfred's little brother as a "backup" hero, attributed his death to Lothar von Richthofen.[37] It seems unlikely that Lothar, who had already tallied sixteen victories, deserved the additional kudos he was given for shooting Ball down, but the propaganda mill required that someone be credited, much as the Royal Air Force (as the RFC and RNAS would become on 1 April 1918) would claim a year later that Canadian Roy Brown had accounted for the Red Baron. A likelier explanation is that Ball became disoriented in the cloud and simply crashed his SE 5 into the ground. There were certainly no bullet wounds on his body.[38] At the time of his death, Ball was officially credited with forty-four victories — twenty-nine (including one balloon) destroyed, six driven down out of control, and nine simply "forced to land."

One would like to know exactly how and when Bishop learned that Ball was either missing, a prisoner or dead, and what his immediate thoughts were, but we are left in the dark about that. Suddenly, he was the top-scoring Imperial ace — one of his ambitions fulfilled. He was due for leave, and on 8 May he flew one patrol in the morning without seeing an enemy aircraft, then left for England, reaching London the next day. News travelled quickly in the RFC and he may have learned something before he left Filescamp. His own score now stood at nineteen — twelve of them (including the balloons) destroyed and seven driven down out of control — and, as he told his father in a letter a week later, "now that Ball is dead I head the list of RFC pilots."[39]

No one else in the RFC was close. A two-seater pilot, Captain F.J.H. Thayre, together with his several observers, had accounted for nine (and would add eleven more before his death on 7 June). Lieutenant James McCudden had shot down five, but for the moment he was out of the race on an instructor's posting, while Lieutenant Edward Mannock had only just begun his rise to glory, with one balloon to his credit. The RNAS pilots on the Western Front were showing more promise. Flight Lieutenant R.S. Dallas (who would add another seventeen before being killed on 1 June 1918) had been credited with fifteen, and Robert Little had accounted for thirteen. Another Canadian, Raymond Collishaw of Nanaimo, British Columbia, claimed the seventh of his eventual sixty victories on 9 May.[40]

Understandably, flying all the hours that he did, Bishop badly needed a rest. Early in May he had told Margaret that "in two weeks I should be going to England on leave.... It will be wonderful to have that feeling that there is really a good chance of living for a few days." Three days later, he had repeated that he was "dead tired."[41] He had written to tell Lady St. Helier that he was coming and had been invited to stay at her Portland Square home.

> I arrived during a dinner party, and spent the evening talking to Princess Mary Louise [he told his father]. She came again Saturday night and I made a great hit. Under the influence of champagne I told her the most brilliant lie of my career. I told her Louie [his sister] was named after her, which so pleased her that Lady St. Helier has today received an order to bring me to see her father, old Prince Christian.[42]

Like many of his biographers, Bishop had not yet got the spelling of the Princess's name quite right — *Mary* Louise, Queen Victoria's fourth daughter, who had married the Marquis of Lorne (later Duke of Argyll), was sixty-nine years old in 1917; *Marie* Louise was a lively divorcée* of forty-five — and not one of those negligible royals who dwelt among the outermost fringes of the *Almanach de Gotha*, either. Seven years younger than gruff cousin George, and less a slave to etiquette than either he or his queen (a second cousin), she brought a ray of sunshine into an essentially austere family.

---

* Her husband, Prince Aribert of Anhalt-Dessau, had summarily dumped her in 1900, after nine years of marriage. Marie Louise apparently lacked the *gravitas* required by a German court.

During the 1914–1918 War, we were in very close touch with him and, of course, Queen Mary [she wrote]. During the summer months of those eventful years, they were usually in residence at Windsor, and my parents and we two sisters were at Cumberland Lodge [in Windsor Great Park]. In consequence, there was a constant coming and going between the Castle and our home. To lunch on Sunday at the Castle was an established fact.[43]

When Marie Louise was not lunching at Windsor Castle, she was calling on her cousins at Buckingham Palace — her visits regularly recorded in *The Times*' Court Circular. No doubt the King soon got to hear about her new friend, this debonair young Canadian who already wore the ribbons of the MC and DSO. (Bishop was notified of the latter award by a telegram from Scott the morning after his arrival at Portland Square.)

"Tomorrow I am asked to lunch with Sir F.E. Smith, the Attorney General, and the night after to dine with Lord Beaverbrook (Sir Max Aitken), so it helps having more Huns to your credit than any other Britisher," he told Margaret as he cut a swathe through London's high society. "There was a dinner party here tonight. Princess Marie Louise is here and about four Lord and Lady Somebody."[44]

"Life has been a round of gayeties [sic]," he reported in another letter, showing a keen eye for character as he labelled Max Aitken, the newly created Lord Beaverbrook, "an old scoundrel."[45] He was not yet a popular hero outside the ranks of the Flying Corps, as Albert Ball was quickly becoming now that he was dead (Ball's influential father had opened a quickly successful public relations campaign to get his son a posthumous VC), but among Bishop's influential new friends who understood the growing importance of public opinion there was surely a sentiment of "The Ace Is Dead; Long Live the Ace."

His leave over, Bishop was back in action (by himself, as Scott noted) on 26 May, notching up another single-seater victim, "the highest and rear machine of a formation of six" that he claimed to have surprised near Izel-les-Esquerchin at a height of 11,500 feet. "I fired 25 rounds from underneath at 50 yds range with my gun down [i.e., with the butt pulled down as for reloading]. The tracers went in his machine under the pilot's seat, and the H. A. fell completely out of control in a spin."[46] The next day, when a patrol he was leading tangled with a German formation, gun trouble sent him home by himself; but that evening, flying alone, he claimed to have shot down a two-seater that crashed in the village of Dourgies for his twenty-first victory. Both combats, if genuine, occurred well behind enemy lines.

On the 30th, he was leading a patrol that was attacked by five unidentified enemy aircraft, presumably single-seaters, when his gun jammed with a broken extractor — not a stoppage that could be corrected in the air — after firing ten fruitless rounds. Since the enemy did not realize that his gun was jammed, he was able to escape unharmed while his comrades held the foe at bay. He claimed another victim on the evening of the 31st, on one of his solitary sorties deep in German airspace. Meeting two enemy scouts, he reported, he "dived from the sun at the back one ... firing about 10 rounds from 50 yds range. He turned and manoeuvred with me for a few seconds. I finally succeeded in getting another burst of 15 rounds in, and he went down out of control. I watched him & he crashed at [map reference near Epinoy]."[47]

On 1 June, Bishop attacked an Albatros two-seater, presumably a C-III, "with no apparent result." The handwritten combat report has a sentence added by Fry — "I dived after Captain Bishop & fired 1/2 of a drum at fairly long range."[48] What is odd about this statement is that, as noted earlier according to his own account, Fry's logbook only ever mentioned one fight he was engaged in together with Bishop — and he only remembered one fight! This was certainly a second. However, it reinforces the point that, all too often when Bishop met the enemy while flying in company, he was unsuccessful. Sometimes, as with the broken extractor, there was good reason for his lack of success; at other times there was no convincing explanation provided in the admittedly curt combat reports that he (and every other pilot) submitted. What they do reveal, of course, is that there were witnesses to his lack of success!

Of course, there was no immutable rule of aerial warfare that said a man could not be significantly more victorious when flying alone than in company. Indeed, "single-seater scouts … if superior in speed and climb to the great majority of the enemy's machines, may be able to patrol very successfully alone or in pairs, taking advantage of their power of manoeuvre and acting largely by surprise."[49] But Bishop's Nieuport was not superior in speed. At a time when team combat had become the norm, a man flying alone was prey for the pack and the odds were heavily against him. He needed to fly cautiously, calculating the risks very carefully, before lunging at an enemy. How many others were in the vicinity, lurking in a nearby cloud or circling high above, up-sun with the advantage of height? If in any doubt, back off. When he was part of a pack, however, the same man could attack with rather more confidence, knowing that his comrades were there in support if he had missed some vital aspect of the situation. Bishop, if he is to be believed, occasionally attacked as many as six enemy machines with confidence, while flying alone.

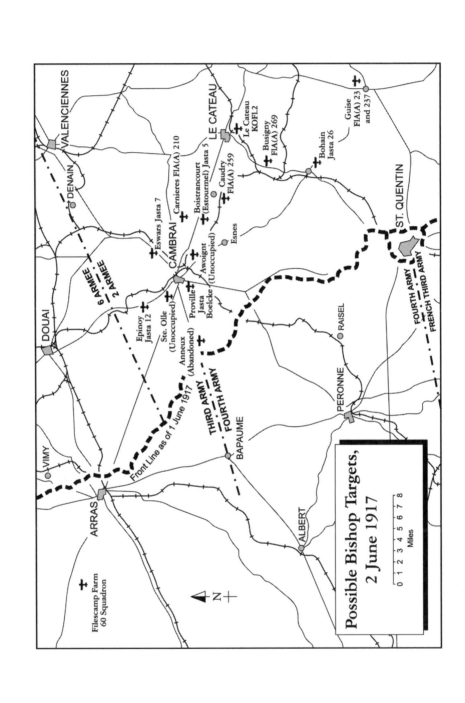

VALENCIENNES

DENAIN

DOUAI

6 ARMEE
2 ARMEE

Epinoy
Jasta 12

Ste. Olle
(Unoccupied)

CAMBRAI

Eswars Jasta 7

Carnieres FIA(A) 210

Boistrancourt
(Estourmel) Jasta 5

LE CATEAU

Le Cateau
KOFL.2

Busigny
FIA(A) 269

Bohain
Jasta 26

Guise
FIA(A) 23
and 237

Caudry
FIA(A) 259

Esnes

Awoignt
(Unoccupied)

Proville
Jasta
Boelcke

ST. QUENTIN

RAISEL

FOURTH ARMY
FRENCH THIRD ARMY

Anneux
(Abandoned)

Front Line as of 1 June 1917

THIRD ARMY
FOURTH ARMY

VIMY

ARRAS

BAPAUME

PERONNE

ALBERT

Filescamp Farm
60 Squadron

N

**Possible Bishop Targets,
2 June 1917**

0 1 2 3 4 5 6 7 8
Miles

CHAPTER 4

Flight of Fancy

Night bombing of airfields had become an established, if ineffective, part of British air strategy in the spring of 1917, but potentially more accurate daylight attacks were apparently not an acceptable option. However tempting the prospect of destroying aircraft on the ground may have been, the possibility of enemy fighters getting into the air, or arriving from other nearby fields in the nick of time, was presumably judged to be too great a threat to the relatively slow, unwieldy bombers.

The idea of fighters strafing airfields in low-level attacks does not seem to have occurred to anyone except Bishop — and possibly Albert Ball, who died before doing anything about it. It would have been a Ball-like thing to do, but in *Winged Warfare* Bishop claimed all the credit for himself. He had carefully calculated that, if he could find a German airfield where machines on the ground were out of their hangars, being prepared for the customary dawn patrol, he could attack them without too much danger to himself. Even if one or two of them succeeded in taking off, he would still have them at a considerable disadvantage: as they struggled to gain height, they would be moving relatively slowly and, superb shot that he was, he should be able to destroy them quite easily in the air. Of course, there remained a significant threat from any enemies who might already be aloft, and these would enjoy a height advantage since the strafing of ground targets would compel Bishop to be low — perhaps no more than a hundred feet above the ground. Getting the timing *exactly* right would be very important: he would need to be late enough to see what he was doing but early enough to catch the enemy still on the ground and unprepared to meet an attack.

He would be flying a machine that had a slightly different engine from any other in the squadron — and, as far as we can tell, from any other in the RFC at that time. The standard Nieuport 17 had a 110 hp J9a motor, but in a letter to Margaret on 18 April Bishop had told her that "I have a beautiful new machine with a glorious new 120 hp engine."[1] The Le Rhône company was then developing the J9a into a new 120 hp engine, the J9b, intended for the short-lived Nieuport 27 that came into limited service later in the summer, and this new engine of Bishop's was probably a prototype. No performance figures exist for a Nieuport 17 fitted with the J9b engine, but the Nieuport 27, when it came into service, had a top speed of 110 mph. But the 17 was 110 lbs lighter than the 27, so it may well be that his new engine gave Bishop's machine a speed of 112 mph. A small but useful advantage, in that it made him marginally faster than an Albatros D-III with its maximum speed of 109 mph.[2]

There would have been a slight increase in fuel consumption, which would have caused a slight reduction in endurance from the J9a's official test-bed figure of 105 minutes at full throttle at ground level.[3] This is an important point. Rotary engines normally operated at full throttle — indeed, the earlier ones could not be used in any way other than "On" or "Off" — the latter state briefly achieved while in the air by means of a "blip" switch. By 1917, more sophisticated carburetors permitted the pilot to cut power by as much as 25 percent by juggling with the air intake valve and fuel lever to readjust the mixture; however, wise pilots made no attempt to do so in the vicinity of the enemy, when any misjudgment could result in the plugs oiling up and a consequent loss of urgently needed power.[4] We can safely assume that Bishop flew at top speed throughout his most famous sortie, so his endurance would have been something less than 105 minutes.

Perhaps he and Ball had planned to go together, in which case one of them could have strafed the airfield while the other kept guard above. But Ball was dead. So Bishop approached his deputy flight commander, Willie Fry, in the course of a TGIF party on the evening of 1 June 1917 to enquire if he would care to join him.

> He said something about shooting up an enemy aerodrome early the next morning and would I care to go with him. I did not take much notice, was non-committal and soon afterwards went to bed. Early the following morning, before light, he came to my room and asked if I were going with him. I had a headache from the night's party and answered that I was not for it, turned over and went to sleep again.[5]

Bishop wrote in *Winged Warfare* that he also spoke to a second — unnamed — member of the squadron (probably Keith Caldwell, the C Flight commander) about accompanying him. If he did so, then he obviously got the same negative response. Did Fry and Caldwell know about Bishop's unique — and superior — engine? It would seem unlikely that they did not, which may well explain their refusals. Had either of them agreed to join in, it would have meant flying an inferi-

or machine that would have put him at even greater risk than Bishop on a sortie that could well prove exceptionally dangerous in any case. Was Bishop's solicitation genuine — did he still seriously intend to attack an enemy airfield when he took off — or did he confidently expect them to refuse, given the additional disadvantage they would have faced? What would he have done had either of them agreed to accompany him? Fascinating questions, which, like so much of this day's story, are impossible to answer more than three-quarters of a century after the fact.

The next morning, according to squadron records, Bishop was in the air at 3:57 a.m. and he landed again 103 minutes later, at 5:40.[6] As we have noted, this is an unlikely, probably impossible, duration, bearing in mind his unusual power plant and the fact that he flew mostly at 1,000 feet or less and, according to his reports, never more than 7,000 feet — that is, not high enough to produce significantly greater endurance. He took off in the near-darkness of nautical twilight on a day when III Brigade weather was reported as "fine in morning but cloudy from noon," while on the German side it was "sunny and hazy early in the morning." Neither friend nor foe mentioned wind at all.[7]

The fullest account of his sortie that we have is found in *Winged Warfare*. There, he wrote that he flew from Filescamp Farm "towards the aerodrome I had planned to attack" — which he identified as Anneux in his reconnaissance report ("recce" reports were prepared to inform higher authority of observations of general interest made during a flight, as opposed to combat reports that detailed any actual fights the reporter engaged in). "But on reaching the place I saw there was nothing on the ground. Everyone must have been either dead asleep, or else the station was absolutely deserted."[8] According to his recce report, it took him fifteen minutes to reach Anneux, about twenty-seven miles from Filescamp — a time that more or less jibes with an airspeed of 110–112 mph, given that he claimed to have been (very sensibly) flying an irregular course, "zagzagging here and there."[9]

If he was over Anneux, then it certainly was "deserted." It had once been well within the great salient that bulged into the Entente lines between Soissons and Arras, but on 15 March the Germans had begun the great voluntary withdrawal, code-named *Alberich*, that straightened their line and shortened it by some thirty miles in a matter of three days. Since 19 March, Anneux had lain less than two miles behind their new front line, within easy range of British heavy artillery. No aircraft could reasonably have been based there under such circumstances, and Bishop and every other RFC flyer on that part of the front (including Jack Scott) must surely have known that. After all, this was the ground that some of them had flown over nearly every day since *Alberich*.

How was it, then, that no one subsequently questioned Bishop's selection of Anneux as his prime target? Did he ever go near it? His recce report noted that, wherever he was, there was "no activity; no machines seen; several sheds,"[10] but made no mention of any damage to the sheds. It seems most unlikely that any of Anneux's sheds would have been intact. It would have been careless of the British artillery, to say the least, not to have ensured that any potential accommodation for men and equipment so close to the front was rendered uninhabitable. It is possible that they had not been totally destroyed, but there would surely have been noticeable damage.

In his report to wing headquarters, received the day after the raid, Scott states that Bishop was "intending to attack the aerodrome at NEUVILLE but on arriving there found the hangars closed and no signs of any activity."[11] The hamlet of Neuville-Vitasse lay close to Anneux, but was Scott perhaps referring to Neuville St. Remy, hard against the airfield known to the Germans as Ste. Olle, just north-west of Cambrai and only very slightly further from Filescamp than Anneux? The sheds there would probably have been undamaged, since the field lay some eight or nine miles behind the front line, and the timing would fit Ste. Olle even better than Anneux. According to the *Wochenberichten* (Weekly Activity Report) of the *Kommandeur der Flieger bein Armeeoberkommando 2* (*KoFl.2*, or 2nd Army Air Commander), Ste. Olle was unoccupied but not abandoned. This report, which lists all the air units in 2 *Armee* area and where they were stationed on 1 June 1917, is one of the few relevant air documents that survived British Second World War bombing.[12]

Both airfields lay alongside dead-straight highways — Anneux on the Cambrai-Bapaume road, Ste. Olle on the Cambrai-Arras road — but while Anneux bordered on the ribbon of desolation that marked the front lines, Ste. Olle flourished in the midst of cultivated fields. A genuine misidentification was hardly possible, and if Bishop had mistakenly written Anneux when he meant Ste. Olle, he could have corrected his error at any later time — certainly when he came to write *Winged Warfare*.

The only other possibility, given Bishop's fifteen-minute timing, was Epinoy, about four miles to the north of Ste. Olle, but Epinoy lay in a much more easterly direction, was occupied by *Jasta 12*, and would almost certainly have been a hive of activity in the pre-dawn moments when Bishop would have arrived there. Since the weather was thoroughly "flyable," ground crew would have been busy preparing their aircraft for the usual dawn patrol; the appearance of a solitary British fighter would have sparked even more intense activity, rather than the "no activity, no machines seen..." documented in Bishop's recce report. The first airfield he reached (if, indeed, he reached any) was surely not Epinoy. All three airfields — Anneux, Ste. Olle and Epinoy — lay in the area of the German Second Army, the army boundary lying just to the north of Epinoy.

"Greatly disappointed, I decided I would try the same stunt some other day on another aerodrome, which I would have to select." In other words, he had now abandoned his plan (if it ever really existed) to attack a working German airfield.

> However, nothing appeared, and I was just thinking
> of turning and going home, or of climbing up to see
> if there were some Huns in the upper sky, when
> ahead, and slightly to one side of me, I saw the sheds
> of another aerodrome. I at once decided that here
> was my chance, although it was not a very
> favourable one, as the aerodrome was pretty far back
> from the lines.... Furthermore, I was not even cer-
> tain where I was, and that was my greatest worry, as
> I was a bit afraid that if I had any bad fights I might
> have trouble finding my way back. Scurrying along
> close to the ground, zagzagging here and there,
> one's sense of direction becomes slightly vague.[13]

Why should he "have trouble finding my way back"? Wherever he might be, he only had to fly due west to reach the Entente lines, and he must have known that.

Both his combat and recce reports identify this second airfield as either Esnes or Awoignt, respectively ten miles to the southeast and eight miles to the east, and he recorded reaching it at 4.25 a.m., which, once again, matches time and distance reasonably well in either case. There was no air unit stationed at Esnes on 1 June 1917, although David Bashow, relying on the work of Bishop apologist Stewart Taylor, argues in his *Knights of the Air* that the airfield Bishop attacked might well have been Esnes, and that the machines he saw were a part of *Jasta 20*, which was in the process of moving from Guise (2 *Armee*) to a new base at Middelburg (4 *Armee*) in Flanders (now a suburb of Oostkamp, four miles south of Brugge and nine or ten miles from the Channel coast) and making an overnight stop en route.[14] But the *Wochenberichten* of KoFl.2 for 24–30 May and 31 May–6 June 1917 (and that of his neighbour, KoFl.6, for 1–7 June)[15] make no mention of *Jasta 20*, although the latter does record the move of *Jasta 26* from 2 *Armee* to 4 *Armee* on 6 June. Moreover, the distance from Guise to Middelburg is only ninety miles, and it was only just over a hundred miles to the Channel coast. The Albatros D-III could stay aloft for two hours at a cruising speed of 90 mph, giving a range of 180 miles. Why would any *Jasta* moving north from 2 *Armee* area have staged overnight at Esnes? There was no need to refuel and there were no theatres or swanky bistros in that tiny French village.

Bashow proposes that because the *Jasta* was on the move between postings, so to speak, this explains the lack of any evidence from the German side of an attack on an airfield. Because the *Jasta* was in transit, he argues, it had no formal administrative superior to report the attack to, although as a serving officer he must surely know that military units are never in administrative limbo. They *always* belong to one formation or another, the changeover usually scheduled to take place at midnight.

Visual clues should have made it clear to Bishop whether he was over Awoignt. Nearly half an hour had passed since he left Filescamp at the moment of nautical twilight — technically (according to *Bowditch's Practical Navigator*) "the period of incomplete darkness when ... the centre of the sun is not more than 12° below the celestial horizon" — or, in layman's terms, when it is still dark enough to see the stars but the horizon is only just becoming visible. Twenty minutes later it would have been twilight at least, verging on fully light, and Awoignt, like Ste. Olle, lay hard against the old, arrow-straight, Roman road that ran from Cambrai to Le Cateau. When he reached there, it would surely have been light enough to see the highway from his low height, and even at that early hour there would probably have been a noticeable amount of traffic using it, bearing in mind that it carried a main German supply line. The troops manning the Arras front needed food and ammunition every day, preferably delivered before it became light enough for balloon observers to direct long-range artillery fire onto the carrier vehicles, or for airmen to bomb or strafe them. If he had reached Awoignt, how could he have any doubts about it?

Finally, we might note, on 1 June Awoignt, like Anneux and Ste. Olle, was unoccupied. There were many such empty fields on the German side, established to handle any sudden influx of *Jastas* required to meet shifting operational commitments.

Wherever Bishop was, thought he was, or may have been, at this second airfield he recorded in his combat report seeing seven aircraft on the ground — in the open, surrounded by mechanics. "Machines on the ground were 6 scouts (Albatros type I or II) and one two-seater."[16] This identification of the single-seaters as Albatros D-Is or IIs is illuminating, for it disposes of Arthur Bishop's assertion that his father attacked Boistrancourt (Arthur calls it Estourmel),[17] which was occupied only by *Jasta* 5 on 1 June, according to *KoFl.2.* The differences between D-IIs and D-IIIs were readily apparent and would certainly have been familiar to Bishop, if only because his first two witnessed victims, at the end of March, had been D-IIs. In plan, the D-II had almost square upper wingtips, while the D-III had tips that curved back to a blunt point toward the trailing edge; seen from an angle or the side, the D-II had vertical inter-plane struts, while the D-III had V-form struts.[18]

It is, of course, possible (but unlikely) that one or two D-IIs had been retained for "recreational" or even operational training purposes, but certainly not six. There was a need for them on other, less sophisticated, fronts — in Russia, Macedonia, Italy and Mesopotamia. There were a number of D-IIs still in service on the Western Front with the larger — nine aircraft each, as opposed to six — *Flieger Abteilungen (Artillerie)* [Fl.A.(A), or Artillery Flying Units]. They were used primarily as close escorts for the C-type two-seaters that carried out the actual artillery observation function, and perhaps, on occasion, to fly reconnaissance sorties, but again it is extremely unlikely that there would be more than three of them with any single *Abteilung*. Since Bishop reported seeing six, that eliminates airfields that currently accommodated only one *Fl.A.(A)*, and the only airfield in 2 *Armee* area in which two such *Abteilungen* were stationed on 1 June was that at Guise, home to *Fl.A.(A) 23* and *Fl.A.(A) 237*. Did Bishop get as far as Guise? It is a question we will return to shortly.

He says that he set about strafing the men and machines on the ground, shooting at least one man. While admiring his handiwork, he came under return fire from the ground and his machine took a number of hits. Then one of the single-seaters took off, and

> … I fired 15 rounds at him from close range 60 feet up and he crashed. A second one taking off, I opened fire and fired thirty rounds at 150 yards range, and he crashed into a tree. Two more were then taking off together. I climbed and engaged one at 1000 feet, finishing my drum, and he crashed 300 yards from the aerodrome. I changed drums and climbed East. A fourth H.A. came after me and I fired one whole drum into him. He flew away…[19]

He would have begun the day with three drums of ammunition, each holding about ninety-five rounds. He never tells us how much ammunition he expended in strafing ground targets before the first Albatros took off, but it seems reasonable to assume that he used up his first drum. His second accounted for his three airborne victims, and the third was fired indecisively at the fourth machine. "… [I]n the course of a short fight, [I] emptied the whole of my last drum at him."[20]

No sooner had he turned away from the airfield and climbed to about 4,000 feet than he found himself flying a thousand feet below four enemy scouts heading south.[21] It would have been very hard for them to see him as long as he stayed directly beneath them, and he maintained that spatial relationship while he mustered up enough courage to break away to the west. Since, by his own report, he had no ammunition left, he might well have been nervous, but the enemy would have found it difficult to see directly below them, and apparently they never did see him.

Now there remained the matter of returning to Filescamp, an issue that did not arise in either his combat or recce reports, but one which is particularly interesting to us if only because backtracking might assist us in discovering exactly where he had been. But, he confessed in *Winged Warfare* — the only account of his return flight that he ever put on paper — he could not tell his readers what route he took home. His version enabled him to avoid any kind of specific statement about anything.

> I now headed in the approximate direction of our
> lines and flew in rather a dazed state towards them.
> I had not had any breakfast, and was feeling very
> queer in my stomach. The excitement, and the
> reaction afterwards, had been a bit too much, as

well as the cold morning air. It seemed, once or twice, that my head was going around and around, and that something must happen. For the only time in my life, it entered my thoughts that I might lose my senses in a moment, and go insane.... I was not at all sure where I was, and furthermore did not care.... nothing seemed to matter but this awful feeling of dizziness and the desire to get home and on the ground.[22]

This self-diagnosed imbroglio of physical distress and psychological despair seems strange and unexplainable in a man who had habitually flown in the cold morning air and been credited with shooting down twenty-two adversaries, half of them before breakfast. However, it conveniently excused him from having to list any topographical features of his return flight which might help identify the field he had attacked.

The only other evidence concerning the return trip comes from his deputy flight commander, Willie Fry, in his memoir *Air of Battle*, and must be slightly suspect after a lapse of more than half a century. Can Fry's memory be trusted? All that can be said in that regard is that, wherever his recollections can be checked against the known facts, they hold up remarkably well.

Fry's account of their conversation, very shortly after Bishop had landed, paints a more detailed and rather different picture of the return flight from that in *Winged Warfare*.

He said he had managed to cross the line further south in the French sector, despite being followed and attacked all the way, had landed in a field behind the French lines to find out where he was, and having got his bearings from some French workers on the land, flew back home. He arrived back without his machine-gun, having undone the screw-up release on the securing collar and thrown the gun overboard after he had let it down on its quadrant to put on a fresh ammunition drum while being attacked on the way home. At that point he had found himself unable to get the new drum on or the gun back into its firing position.[23]

Bishop, it will be remembered, claimed in *Winged Warfare* to have used up all his ammunition before leaving the vicinity of the enemy airfield. Fry, in a book published fifty-seven years later, clearly recalled being told that Bishop had to fight his way home; but if that were so, there should certainly have been some reference to this fight or fights in his combat report. Unfortunately, there is not.

There are other significant differences between Bishop's account and Fry's recollection. Bishop made no mention of jettisoning his gun in *Winged Warfare*, although Fry remembers him explaining not only that he had done so, but why and how. Strangely, no one who saw Bishop's machine immediately after his return seems to have remarked on the absence of his gun, which should surely have attracted some attention. Moreover, RFC headquarters was required to submit to GHQ a "Weekly Machine Gun Return"; that dated 6 June 1917 shows only two Vickers and four Lewis guns lost throughout the RFC in the past week, all of them from machines that had been shot down over enemy lines, and none of them from 60 Squadron.[24]

This evidence contradicts Fry's recollection, but is hardly conclusive. Anyone with military service knows very well that good (i.e., successful) commanding officers and quartermasters or engineering officers take precautions against the fickle finger of fate where accountable stores are concerned. From time to time, they acquire surplus, unaccounted, bits and pieces of such stores by various and sometimes nefarious means. Guns might be damaged, perhaps by shrapnel, and be written off rather than sent for repair. If some parts were salvageable, judicious saving or trading could result in the creation of a whole "spare," which would come in handy the day when misfortune struck, a gun was stolen or mislaid, and an unauthorized replacement was needed. Bishop's missing gun — if it really was missing — could well have been replaced in such a fashion, so the question remains moot.

Fry recalled that Bishop told him he had to land to find out where he was. Attempting to discredit Fry on this point, Bishop supporters have argued that he could not have landed and then taken off again without assistance, but that is certainly not true. Eric Crundall recounts (in a rather different context) how he started his Sopwith Pup (which had a LeRhône J9a engine) and took off entirely unassisted after the machine had spent a cold February night in the open.

> I pegged down the tail, put a petrol can in front of each wheel, turned on the petrol, set the engine controls to "suck-in" position, and rotated the propeller about six times. Then I switched the engine to "contact" and swung the propeller several times but the engine would not start. This is where my rubber tube came in useful. I sucked petrol into it, some of which went into my mouth, and blew the remainder into each of the nine cylinders, via their exhaust valves. Switching on to "contact", and setting the petrol fine

adjustment half open and throttle nearly closed, I swung the propeller again. After a few turns the engine started and continued to "tick over" slowly.

Getting into the machine I taxied to a fairly even surface ... and got into the air.[25]

Starting a still-warm engine on a balmy summer morning would have been much easier and less physically unpleasant. No need to prime each individual cylinder, getting a mouthful of fuel each time.

Inspecting Bishop's machine immediately after he landed, Fry recollected "clearly seeing a group of about five bullet holes in the rear half of the tailplane within a circle of not more than five inches at most."[26] In his addendum to Bishop's combat report, Scott noted that "his machine is full of holes caused by machine gun fire from the ground." In *Winged Warfare*, Bishop himself claimed that, "Everywhere it [his machine] was shot about, bullet holes being in almost every part of it, although none, luckily, within two feet of where I sat. Parts of the machine were so badly damaged as to take a lot of repairing."[27] However, his logbook shows that, that afternoon, he flew the same aircraft, B1566, about fifty miles south to pay a visit on some of his friends at another airfield.* Non-structural damage was relatively simple to repair on a linen-covered frame, but if there were "holes in almost every part" that took "a lot of repairing" when he landed, it seems odd that the plane was fit for joyriding that same afternoon. Fry's account jibes best with the above facts.

A month later, responding to a telephoned request from his immediate superior (apparently Pretyman had requested additional information for the War Office's VC investigation, discussed in the next chapter), Caldwell — the acting commanding officer while

---

* In fact, he flew north, to 54 Sqn at Bray Dunes, east of Dunkirk. Fifty miles south would have taken him into the French lines.

Scott was on leave — listed the damage done to B1566 on 2 June as "17 bullet holes. Trailing edge of lower plane [aileron?] shot away in two bays."[28] Yet another version comes from ex-Sergeant A.A. Nicod, who, as the senior member of his ground crew, would probably have been the first person to see the machine upon Bishop's return and would certainly have had a closer acquaintanceship with it than anyone else. He remembered that there were "a dozen bullet holes in the radius of a few inches just behind his head as he sat in the cockpit."[29] No one else reported specific damage to the fuselage, however, and perhaps Nicod, clinging to the coattails of a hero and enjoying his fifteen minutes of fame, shifted the location of the damage in order to further dramatize Bishop's heroic stature.

How many holes were there — five, twelve, seventeen, or "full of holes"? In the wing, fuselage, or tailplane? In one place, two, three, or everywhere? Two of the five accounts recall the holes as being in exceptionally tight groupings, and Fry, with his usual cautious reserve, remarked only that "whatever machine was on his tail must have been very close indeed to achieve this group."[30] Subsequently, in a letter to Phil Markham recording some of his private thoughts, he referred to "powder marks [a]round holes in elevator,"[31] clearly implying that the range from which the gun had been fired was no more than two or three feet. If the gunner, in the air or on the ground, was "leading" his target correctly at a realistic range (seventy yards or so), as he almost certainly would have been trying to do, the bullets might be spaced relatively closely — the exact distance apart depending on the skill of the gunner, but unlikely to be less than six inches. Whether fired from the ground or from another aircraft, the bullets could be expected to leave holes in a roughly straight line, not in a circular grouping, as Fry recalled. A five-inch grouping such as he claims to have seen could only result from firing on *a stationary target* from very close range. Even a fixed gun firing at a stationary target would scarcely produce so tight a grouping at more than fifty yards' range, since miniscule variations in the quantity of powder in each mass-produced cartridge, and the vibration of the gun itself, would cause some spread of shot.

Finally, under no conceivable circumstances could bullets fired in anger from the ground or another aircraft have left powder marks on the recipient's fabric. So if Fry's recollections were correct, Bishop did, as he apparently told Fry, land somewhere behind the French lines. And it would seem likely that he then turned off his engine, detached his Lewis gun from its mounting, fired a short burst into one of the less vital parts of B1566 from his hand-held gun, and then (with no time to spare, since he wanted his engine warm for easier starting) failed to remount the gun, chucked it aside, and taken off again, all within six or seven minutes. That is the scenario that comes closest to matching the evidence.

As for those key thirty-five minutes that Bishop allegedly spent fighting Albatroses over the second airfield he visited, whatever he did, he did not spend the time shooting down enemy aircraft. One opponent, he claimed, crashed from a height of sixty feet, one was barely off the ground and the third crashed from a greater height — from a thousand feet, if RFC Communiqué Number 91 is correct. A lucky pilot might have survived the first or second impacts with minor injuries not worth reporting, but at least one of the three would surely have been significantly injured, if not killed.

However, the Weekly Activity Report of *KoFl.2* does not record anyone as killed, injured or missing on 2 June. Nor can there be any question of the reporting system being a day or two behind the events concerned, for no one was recorded as killed, injured or missing on the 3rd, either; only on the 4th do we find "*Leutnant* Köppe (observer), *Fl.A.(A) 269,* killed in aerial combat." Köppe was obviously in a two-seater, and Bishop claimed his three victims were all single-seaters.

In a book entitled *Courage in the Air* (a compendium of notable feats in aerial war which came out after *The Courage of the Early Morning*), Arthur Bishop claims that the raid was "[c]onfirmed by Spencer Horn, a member of Bishop's flight who, with two other pilots, flew over the field [Estourmel ?] in the morning and surveyed the damage."[32] This is nonsense. The Squadron Record Book shows that Horn did not fly at all on 2 June 1917, although he flew three sorties on 1 June and three on 3 June.[33] But in such nefarious ways are legends made.

Dan McCaffery, in his *Billy Bishop, Canadian Hero*, provides a list of all Bishop's alleged victories, and includes "the identities of dozens of Allied servicemen who confirmed his kills,"[34] thus lending his total an air of authenticity. But nearly all his witnesses are highly suspect at best and demonstrably false at worst. His nominee for the confirmation of Bishop's claims on 2 June, Lieutenant Philip Townsend, provides an excellent example. Townsend was stationed at Boistrancourt in October/November 1918 (when, of course, the British had advanced well beyond that point), and he recalled in a 1985 letter to *Cross & Cockade* being told (by whom is not established) that "a British scout had attacked the German aircraft [sic] one morning in 1917 and shot down three Huns."[35]

That would only be vague, third-hand evidence at best, from a witness who probably had every reason to oblige this curious British officer. But before his death in 1991, Townsend assured Phil Markham that he had clearly explained to McCaffery (when the latter contacted him to confirm the recollection in his letter) that he was only repeating hearsay.[36] Where and when this hearsay occurred, he did not specify. Like Arthur Bishop, in a later book McCaffery attempted to strengthen his case by claiming that "Allied agents behind the [German] lines had been able to confirm the story, even finding out that the two-seater that never got off the ground had been badly damaged and had to be totally rebuilt."[37] However, he offers no source for his unlikely tale.

On the other hand, another strong piece of evidence refuting Bishop's claim to even as much as strafing an airfield, never mind shooting down three enemies, is the next section of the *KoFl.2* report. "In general terms, no changes were noted with regard to changes in the type and intensity of enemy air activity," wrote the *Kommandeur*. "The airfield of Jagdstaffel Boelcke [Proville] was bombed during the nights of 3/4 and 5/6 June; no damage was inflicted."[38] Night bombing of airfields was not that uncommon but still rated a mention. The daylight strafing of an airfield would have been unique and would certainly have been heralded as a change — a most significant change. It would have been important to alert all subordinates to the possibility that their airfield might be the next to be attacked in daylight, when the likelihood of damage would be much greater than at night. But there is no mention of any such episode by *KoFl.2*.

Let us now review the questions of timings and aircraft types, central in assessing the validity of Bishop's story. We know from squadron records that he took off at 3:57 a.m. and landed again at 5:40, so that he was away for 103 minutes.[39] According to his own reports, presumably noted from the clock that occupied a prominent place on his simple, uncluttered instrument panel, he took fifteen minutes to reach his initial objective — which he said was the

abandoned field at Anneux, although the unabandoned (but unoccupied) one at Ste. Olle seems more likely. There was a solitary
Fl.A.(A) at Busigny, about nineteen miles from Anneux, which he
could have reached in fractionally more than ten minutes, but his
claim of *six* single-seaters on the ground makes Busigny improbable
unless there was a number of overnight visitors for some undiscov-
ered and unlikely reason. Bohain, eighteen miles south of Anneux,
housed *Jasta 26*, so the aircraft types there would not match up with
Bishop's report. Finally, Guise, where there were two *Fl.A.(A)*s stationed, possibly with six D-Is or D-IIs between them, lay some twen-
ty-eight miles southeast of Anneux and would have taken him
another seventeen minutes to reach.

There are really only conceivable three possibilities — Awoignt,
Boistrancourt or Guise. Let us look at the timings for each of these
three scenarios.

Filescamp Farm to Anneux or Ste. Olle	15 mins.
Observing the field, say	2 mins.
Anneux/Ste. Olle to Awoignt (unoccupied on 2 June)	6 mins.
Time spent there	35 mins.
Flying south for approximately one mile	less than 2 mins.
Flying due west until across the lines, say	8 mins.
Direct return to Filescamp	17 mins.
Approximate time aloft	85 mins.

Eighty-five minutes deducted from the 103 that he was away
from Filescamp leaves 18 minutes unaccounted for. Even if he had
landed behind the French lines to find out where he was, that need
not have taken more than half of the unaccounted minutes. Or did
he spend time chatting up a French peasant farmer — or the
farmer's daughter?

Filescamp to Anneux or Ste. Olle	15 mins.
Observing the field, say	2 mins.
Anneux/Ste. Olle to Boistrancourt (Jasta 5 — D-IIIs)	9 mins.
Time spent strafing and fighting	35 mins.
Flying south for approximately one mile	less than 2 mins.
Flying due west until across the lines, say	11 mins.
Direct return to Filescamp	18 mins.
Approximate time aloft	92 mins.

Eleven minutes unaccounted for, conceivably attributable to landing to discover where he was, although such a time still seems somewhat excessive. Assuming that he did land, an attack on Boistrancourt can be reconciled with the time he was away from Filescamp, but the claim that he saw and attacked Albatros D-IIs does not agree with the type of aircraft that we know were the only ones based there on 2 June.

Filescamp to Anneux or Ste. Olle	15 mins.
Observing the field, say	2 mins.
Anneux or Ste. Olle to Guise (Fl.A(A) 23 and Fl. A(A) 237 — D-IIs)	17 mins.
Time spent strafing and fighting	35 mins.
Flying south for approximately one mile	less than 2 mins.
Flying due west across the lines	12 mins.
Direct return to Filescamp	32 mins.
Approximate time aloft	115 mins.

An attack on Guise fits with the type of aircraft but involves absolutely impossible timing — his machine could not have been aloft that long on one tank of fuel.

We are left to consider the deplorable alternative that Bishop never went near a German airfield but simply followed the front lines south, probably on the German side of the front. Somewhere,perhaps, he turned west and landed in a field well back from the French lines and well away from inconvenient busybodies, shot up his own machine and, unable to remount the gun, abandoned it and flew home. That scenario allows for the fact that his fuel tank was not absolutely dry when he returned to Filescamp 103 minutes after leaving that fateful morning.

Let us also note that, although cynics may choose to dismiss it as German counter-propaganda, the *Nachrichterblatt der Luftstreitkräfte* [Air Service news sheet], Number 37 of 8 November 1917, commenting on a report of Bishop's feat that had just appeared in the French press, noted that, "Since Bishop was alone in the fight, details of this *fictitious* incident [my emphasis] can only have come from him."

The only thing that we can be absolutely sure of is that events did not unfold as he claimed. The certain truth seems beyond recovery eighty-odd years after the fact and after the destruction of so many of the German records, but there is too much contrary evidence, and too many inconsistencies and contradictions, for a reasonable man to believe Bishop's account of his VC–winning raid on 2 June 1917.

CHAPTER 5

Flying High

Jack Scott was undoubtedly thrilled by Bishop's account of his morning's work. "After breakfast, when he [Bishop] had time to recover, the CO obtained the details from him in some sequence and a combat report was made out."[1] Scott then began to telephone his friends and superiors. One of the first to hear must have been Brigadier General Higgins at III Brigade, who wrote the recommendation for a Victoria Cross dated that same day. Higgins should have been the first or second reviewing authority, and not the originator of this nomination. That was properly Scott's job, but perhaps his first attempt, three weeks earlier, had failed to produce the intended result. Possibly Higgins could do better. Scott stood three ranks lower in the military hierarchy and was, in the final analysis, only a wartime soldier. The first Regular in the chain of command was Pretyman, but he was very young for his rank. It would seem that they all three felt that a recommendation originating with Higgins would carry more weight in the corridors of power.

The next authority required to endorse the recommendation was the commander of the Third Army, Sir Edmund Allenby. He probably received Higgins' submission the next day, but even if it had arrived that same evening it would have been no surprise to him. Readers may recall that his military secretary was Lord Dalmeny, an old friend of Scott's from the pre-war era, and Dalmeny was an early recipient of one of those phone calls on the 2nd. "Major Scott called him soon after Bishop's return and was invited to take him over to see the Army Commander who wanted to hear his story at first hand," according to Willie Fry, who was himself awaiting the result of Scott's efforts to get him a Military Cross (it was promulgated a few days later) and was probably included in the party for that reason. "I was taken too, and after Bishop had told his story to the Army Commander we had luncheon in one of the Headquarters messes."[2]

Trenchard was the air adviser to Sir Douglas Haig, and not an operational commander, which put him out of the direct chain of endorsement. However, Scott also telephoned him on the 2nd, and Trenchard promptly signalled his congratulations to Bishop, and probably had a word with Haig very shortly afterwards. Certainly, a version of Bishop's combat report, probably dictated over the telephone, was in Haig's hands (at St. Omer, thirty miles north of Filescamp) that same day, and the next morning the commander-in-chief personally annotated it. "A fine performance. Hearty Congratulations. D. H."[3]

In due course, Higgins' formal submission must also have crossed Haig's desk, to be endorsed once more and forwarded to the War Office committee responsible for reviewing VC recommendations before the file was passed to the monarch. Normally, this was no perfunctory, lackadaisical process. The committee's first task, after its constitution in late 1914, had been to examine the twenty-four recommendations for awards submitted since the outbreak of war. Eleven had been quickly approved, but the remaining cases had been referred back to the originators with a request for more details "than in the brief notes submitted ..."[4]

From time to time the committee still found it necessary to ask for additional information. Almost certainly, the unrecorded telephone message to 60 Squadron that resulted in Caldwell, as acting CO, responding on paper that the basis for the award was "personal evidence only" was the result of such a request. Regrettably, however, we know nothing of the committee's deliberations that resulted in the submission being passed to the monarch even though it clearly failed to meet the usual standards.

It should be noted that the corroboration of witnesses was not an absolute necessity. The eighth ordinance of the original Royal Warrant had only specified that "where such act shall not have been performed in sight of a Commanding Officer then the claimant for the honour shall prove the act to the satisfaction of the Officer Commanding the Regiment to which the claimant belongs," while the reviewing authority "shall call for such description and attestation of the act as he may think requisite." In other words, if the reviewing authority felt that no more proof was required, he was free to forward the recommendation as it stood. Even the 1920 General Revision of the Warrant only required COs to call for "conclusive proof *as far as the circumstances of the case will allow* [my emphasis]."

Haig's approval may have been coaxed from him by Trenchard's explaining how badly the RFC needed a morale boost at this particular point in time, but the London committee should not have been so easily convinced. In the summer of 1917 it consisted of the permanent undersecretary of state for war, Sir R.H. Brade (a civil servant); the military secretary to the War Office, Lieutenant General Sir F.J. Davies; the deputy chief of the general staff, Major General Sir Robert Whigham; and a nominee of the adjutant general, Lieutenant General Sir C.F.N. Macready. Whether the fourth member was Macready himself or a subordinate, it would certainly have been an officer of general rank. Why did none of them demand more confirmation? Witnesses may not have been the rule, but they were certainly the custom.

The only answers that come to mind is that they, too, had been made aware of the need to stimulate RFC morale, or that more than one member of the committee (and perhaps all of them) were being subtly pressured by London society, or both. Lady St. Helier would certainly have heard from Scott about Bishop's flight and the VC submission long before word reached London through official channels, and she would have passed the news to Churchill, F.E. Smith, Hugh Cecil and many another influential crony. Genteel indoctrination over the teacups or wineglasses would soon have made committee members aware that a great many important people knew of, and were greatly interested in the fortunes of, the gallant and perfectly charming young Canadian.

Among those told at a very early stage would have been St. Helier's dear friend, Princess Marie Louise, who, as we have noted, lunched with the royal family at Windsor nearly every Sunday during the summer. It is inconceivable that Bishop's name was not mentioned at more than one of those meals as a matter of both public and personal interest. The fact that the alleged raid had taken place on 2 June, which was also the King's birthday, would have provided a convenient starting point.

All this is speculation. It has to be. Crook writes of "the virtually complete weeding (i.e., destruction) of all War Office files on First World War VC awards from 1915 on."[5] Phil Markham made his own enquiries, trying to find out more about their fate, and met with two rather different stories. He was told by one Ministry of Defence bureaucrat in 1986 that they "were destroyed sometime since the end of World War II," but in 1993 another official explained that "the Germans dropped a bomb … on the building containing many old files and … some of the files destroyed may have been those containing the World War I VC papers."[6] The second explanation would seem to be more likely. If the files had been weeded, why retain the papers for 1914 but not those for later awards? Whatever the case, it seems improbable that we shall ever find out more about the confirmation process.

The morning after his VC–winning exploit, Bishop led a patrol that saw some enemy machines but failed to engage them. Then, in the afternoon, "I had to … go up after a Hun who was playing about," he told Margaret. In fact, he flew two solo sorties and on both occasions reported seeing the enemy but not closing with him. On the 4th, he led a patrol of five machines, including those of Fry and Horn, which became involved in three fruitless engagements. "When flying alone, on a day off or something like that, I took queer chances, it is true," he wrote in *Winged Warfare*, "but flying with the patrol often let opportunities slip by because they were not quite good enough, but when the right ones came we were quick to seize them and were nearly always successful."[7] Not this time, however.

On the 6th, he reported to Margaret that "Sir Max Aitken (Lord Beaverbrook) has written suggesting that he has two extraordinarily good jobs in the Canadian Flying Corps when it is formed, for Major Scott and myself. I told Scott I'll do whatever he does." This was Bishop's first reference to the organization that would eventually take him away from the front line for good. Now that Sir Edward Kemp had succeeded Sam Hughes as minister of militia and defence and an Overseas Ministry had been established in London, a proposal for a Canadian air force was coming under consideration.

On the 7th, while he was leading his flight again, they met up on two occasions with enemy aircraft, but "they ran like stuck pigs whenever we approached and we didn't have a fight."[8] The next day, however, while flying alone, he reported four clashes in the course of two sorties. The first of them he described as occurring north of Lille, four or five miles over the enemy lines. "I attacked the 2 top machines in a layer formation of six scouts. I got on the tail of one and fired the remainder of my drum, about 45 rounds, at him. He fell out of control. I watched and he kept spinning all the way down & seemed to go straight into the ground."[9] Scott credited him with yet another Albatros D-III for his twenty-sixth victory, but there are strange and difficult aspects to this story. In *Winged Warfare* he notes that "the other machine of the top layer saw me, but had no desire to fight, and dived away immediately towards the rest of the formation."[10] However, it seems unlikely that all five survivors, who could hardly have missed seeing their comrade fall, would have totally ignored his attacker and simply flown off about some other business. After all, *Jasta* pilots were there primarily to pick fights whenever they had an edge.

Moreover, Bishop was taking a very "queer chance" indeed in watching his victim fall all that way. "It is well if you are against odds never to stay long after one machine," he subsequently wrote in *Winged Warfare*. "If you concentrate on him for more than a fraction of a second, some other Hun has a chance to get a steady shot at you."[11] But in this case, the confrontation took place at 11,500 feet, and to track the falling Albatros visually, right down to the ground more than two miles below, would have required him to concentrate his attention on it. Spinning down, it would have taken five minutes or more to reach the unyielding earth and, even if the remainder of the enemy formation had flown away, no pilot in his right mind would have spent that length of time watching his victim fall while flying alone, far over the German lines, in the general vicinity — by his own account — of at least five other hostile fighters.

On 15 June, the whole of C Flight joined in attacking a solitary two-seater over Boiry Notre Dame. "I fired one drum, Lieut. Fry 70 rounds, Lt. Rutherford 1/2 drum, Lieut. Lloyd 30 rounds," but nevertheless their opponent "went down to 500 ft and flew away E[ast], not returning."[12] When Bishop flew alone, he often seemed able to bring down a victim with fifteen or twenty rounds, but when in company with others he could just as easily fire off a whole drum without success. On the 24th, while leading his flight, he again "fired one drum" at an Albatros D-III which simply flew away; but, later that day while flying alone, he claimed his twenty-seventh victory by "firing about 20 rounds diagonally through the fuselage of an 'old type' Albatros"[13] — presumably a D-II on the strength of a reinforced *Flieger Abteilung (A)*.

On that same 24 June, Lieutenant Gladstone Murray, another Canadian (and a pre-war Rhodes scholar) who had been flying BE 2d two-seaters in 7 Squadron, finished his tour and was posted to the Home Establishment.[14] Forty years later, after he had retired as head of the Canadian Broadcasting Corporation, he was quoted in one of those "gee-whiz" magazine articles recounting Bishop's auspicious career as a fighter pilot.

> ... my first meeting with Billy Bishop was in the air and in action, between Armentieres and Lille, in France, after the Battle of Messines in 1917. I was on a reconnaissance and photography job and got cut off from our lines by a group of six German scouts. Suddenly there appeared a Nieuport [which], as if by magic, dipped his right wing twice and promptly dispersed the Germans, sending two of them down

in flames. A few days later I had the pleasure of meeting Billy Bishop on the ground and discovered it was he who dipped his wing and saved me.[15]

A dramatic authentication of two Bishop victories from a distinguished Canadian of indisputable integrity! Unfortunately, it cannot be reconciled with the facts. The Battle of Messines ended on 14 June, so that the incident described by Murray must have occurred between that date and the 24th, the day Murray was posted to the Home Establishment and left for England. True, Bishop claimed one machine that "burst into flames" while flying alone on the 24th, but that was near Beaumont, many miles away. Otherwise (and unusually) he made no claims at all during those ten days — much of the time the squadron was concluding its conversion to SE 5s — and only on 13 August would he claim two flamers in one sortie.

On 27 June, Major Scott went off on ten days' home leave and Caldwell, by virtue of his seniority, became the acting squadron commander. Although Bishop was flying about as much as usual, there was a sudden paucity of claims on his part until Scott returned. The next morning was a cloudy one and, while flying part of the time in company with Caldwell, Bishop reported an unsuccessful attack on an otherwise unidentified enemy aircraft east of Lens, then two unsuccessful attacks on a two-seater in the vicinity of Henin-Liètard. Still on the same sortie, after parting from Caldwell, "I saw a scout & two-seater. I attacked the former & fired 20 rounds at long range. He flew E[ast], then dived down, apparently about to land. I then dived on the two-seater, finishing my drum at 300x [yards? feet?] range. He flew E. and did not return."[16]

In his logbook he recorded the scout as "shot down out of control." In Scott's absence it was Caldwell's job to assess the damage, and he categorized it, fairly enough in light of the combat report wording, as "1 indecisive." But by the time the engagement was recorded in RFC Communiqué Number 94, Bishop had "attacked a German machine which fell o[ut] o[f] c[ontrol] and broke to pieces before crashing" for his thirty-first victory.

A letter to Margaret told her that when Scott returned from leave:

> I am going to apply for a special machine. I think the general will give me one if Scott will forward the application. It will mean dozens more Huns for me, I'm sure. On an SE 5 or a Spad with a 200 hp engine one could shoot down every Hun in the sky, I'm sure. I can hardly wait until he gets back before applying.[17]

A convenient spell of bad weather stopped flying for nearly all the time that Scott was away and gave Bishop a much-needed rest. Another letter reported that when Scott returned:

> … he will know more about the [proposed] Canadian Flying Corps and when it is to be formed. Then I will have a better idea of when I will be back. In any case, I don't suppose my nerves will last me more than three months more out here. They are getting shaky now. I find myself shuddering at chances I didn't think of six weeks ago.[18]

The idea of a Canadian Flying Corps was being pushed by Sir George Perley, the high commissioner in London and head of the Overseas Ministry, and the newly knighted General Sir Richard Turner, general officer commanding Canadian Forces in the British Isles. Prime Minister Sir Robert Borden blew hot and cold.

The British government, of course, was firmly against it, since if all the Canadians in the RFC were concentrated in a Canadian air force it would significantly weaken the former organization, not to mention the RNAS.[19] It was an issue that would not be settled for another year, and when Scott returned on 7 July, he bore no news of it — only that he was to be promoted and take command of a wing in the near future.

Bishop's next claim came on 10 July, when:

> I led the patrol diving on 7 scouts. I opened fire 6 or 7 times, firing bursts of about 15 rounds from ranges varying from 15 yds to 200 yds. One scout into which I fired 15 rounds at 75 yds range went out of control in a spin. I was unable to watch him owing to other combats, although I saw him still spinning about 3,000 ft under us. During the combat Capt. [sic] Scott engaged a Hun who was opening fire on me from close range. Later the patrol dived on two scouts who dived to the ground.[20]

There was more to it than that, however. "Scott had landed back at 8.25 p.m., after thirty minutes in the air, having been wounded and his aircraft so badly damaged that it barely got him back to base. Mechanics pulled him out of the cockpit with blood running down his sleeve, and rushed him off to hospital."[21]

That was the last the squadron would see of their enthusiastic mentor, who, after being awarded an MC for his efforts and recovering sufficiently from his wound, would take up an appointment as 11th (Army) Wing commander. His replacement was a newly promoted twenty-one-year-old, Major W.J.C. Kennedy-Cochran-Patrick, MC, considered by Trenchard to be "the most brilliant pilot at the front."[22] A Bar to his MC and a DSO were both gazetted within a few weeks of his arrival at Filescamp.

For the first week of this new régime, Bishop flew mostly in company, leading his flight while he took the measure of his new CO. Things might have changed drastically, but in the event, he had no need to worry. The youthful Kennedy-Cochran-Patrick would not engage in the kind of active promotional role that had been Scott's, but neither would he make any attempt to rein Bishop in. What was good enough for Pretyman, Higgins and Trenchard would be good enough for him.

Leading a patrol, Bishop was credited with yet another D-III "crashed" on the 12th, when its pilot "had the impudence to loop directly under me." His opponent must have been a novice, for experienced pilots *never* looped in combat. A machine upside down and moving relatively slowly at the top of a loop, unable for the moment to take any evasive action, was exceptionally vulnerable — rather like a hockey player skating along the blue line with his head down. In this case Bishop would have played the part of the on-rushing defenceman. "I happened to be diving just as he reached the top of the loop, and as he was coming out of it I got a direct shot on to the bottom of his machine," he wrote.

> Another machine had now joined the fight — a machine from one of our naval squadrons stationed in France, and he also was doing very well as I saw a machine which he fired at, fall out of control.... We returned home, and I waved to our new acquaintance from the naval squadron, so he followed me back to the aerodrome and landed beside me to tell me that he had also seen my machine crash. It turned out that this man was the

one who was leading the naval flyers and was next
to me, at that time, in the number of machines
which had been brought down by an Englishman
then in France.[23]

His new acquaintance was an Australian, Flight Commander
Robert Little of "Naval Eight," and that was his twenty-fifth victory
out of the forty-seven he would accumulate before being shot down
and killed on 27 May 1918. Bishop's was his thirty-third, and the III
Brigade daily summary took the trouble to note that "its crash was
confirmed by fellow pilots."[24] This was only the third occasion when
eyewitness confirmation of a Bishop claim was recorded. The next
day his patrol "attacked 1 E.A. which escaped. I fired 15 rounds, Lt.
Young 1 drum, Lt. Horn 1 drum."[25] Another undated combat report
from this time records how "the patrol followed a 2-seater above us,
& climbed up to within 700 feet of it. I fired 40 rounds from underneath with no result. He escaped."

Four days later he noted in his logbook that "about 20 E.A. seen
(many engaged by patrol): 4 engaged, one shot down in flames and 1
out of control."[26] The mention of a patrol makes it appear that these
two successes were claimed while he was flying in company, but that
was not the case according to his logbook. Patrols were normally identified in its pages as either "DOP" or "COP" — shorthand for Distant
or Close Offensive Patrol — and sometimes as DP for Defensive
Patrol. Whenever he flew alone, it was noted as simply "EA" — presumably an abbreviation for "in search of Enemy Aircraft." This flight
was listed as an "EA." He was flying alone, although the patrol, aloft at
the same time and possibly in his general vicinity, may have seen and
attacked some of the same enemy machines.

On 20 July, he reported taking on five opponents and forcing
one down "completely out of control" for his thirty-sixth alleged vic-

tory, and his last flying Nieuport B1566. The squadron had received its first SE 5 — so labelled by Bishop, but more probably an SE 5a with its 200 hp engine — for practice purposes on 8 July and would not be fully re-equipped until the end of August.[27] Bishop, of course, had been the first pilot to get one, and he had been taking it up, getting fully comfortable with it, for the past few days.

The SE 5a could not climb quite as fast as the Nieuport, and was certainly less nimble, but it was structurally sounder, noticeably faster in level flight, and provided a more stable gun platform. It also boasted *two* guns: a drum-fed Lewis over the upper wing, mounted on a Foster quadrant high enough to permit it to fire along the line of flight; and a synchronized, belt-fed Vickers on the left side of the engine cowling. With a maximum speed of 119 mph at 6,500 feet, the SE could outrun the Albatros D-III, still the standard German fighter, and match it in every other respect except ceiling, where the D-III still enjoyed an advantage of about 1,000 feet.[28]

Not until 23 July, when the squadron had six of them on strength, were the pilots sufficiently confident to fly their new machines in harm's way. In the event, they were overconfident. There was a problem with the new Constantinescu interrupter gear for the Vickers machine gun which worked on a hydraulic principle as opposed to the mechanical gears of earlier systems. It needed careful adjustment and the squadron mechanics had difficulty with it. The squadron's first sorties left much to be desired, even though (as Bishop wrote to his father on the 24th) "we haven't crossed the lines with them yet." Just the day before, he had "fired forty rounds at 300 yds at one of 2 E.A. who immediately re-crossed the lines, diving away. Owing to orders I was unable to follow."

The account he gave to Margaret was more graphic. "Tonight we did our first jobs on SE 5s and my gun was the only one that fired, and it shot holes in my propeller, and it will take days to get a new one, so I am thoroughly fed up with life tonight." The following day, "an expert came over to see about the gear for firing our guns on the SE 5s and ever since he arrived he has been working like fury on my machine. Last night I put 9 bullet holes in my propeller again, so another one is done in."[29] However, there would be no more complaints of faulty synchronization.

On 26 July, he was complaining to Margaret that "a whole week has gone by and I haven't got a Hun," but his first victory in the new machine was claimed two days later.

> Seeing 3 E.A. flying N[orth] E[ast], I left the patrol to catch them. I attacked them from the rear, firing on one from 200 yds range. After 20 rounds from each gun he burst into flames. One of the remaining 2 then dived away, the 3rd not having stayed in the fight at all. I dived after him, firing 50 rounds from my Vickers & 30 from the Lewis without result.[30]

Bishop's thirty-eighth victim fell "completely out of control" while he was flying alone on the 29th. But he had not started out alone.

> Caldwell, Gunner and myself all went out on our SEs, and we crossed the Hun lines [at] about 9,000 ft. A machine (Hun) doing artillery registration was just a speck in the distance. It must have been signalled to [by some observers on the ground] that SE 5s were on the way, because it dived all the way to the ground. It was ludicrous, as these two-seaters usually fight. Then four Hun scouts saw us, and came down out of the sky at us. When 300 yds away they saw we were SEs and turned to flee.

Caldwell and I opened out and caught them. I opened fire with my two guns and every time I fired the Huns would dive away.... If I saw one Hun getting above the rest, over to one side, I flew across at 130 miles an hour and opened fire and he would duck again. Both Caldwell's guns jammed and he had to leave.

Three more Huns joined the original four and Gunner lost his way or something and I was left alone....

When they were three against four, nothing decisive had happened, but now that it was *one against seven*, success was imminent

... I shot down one and kept the rest under my thumb for 15 minutes. Then, as I was drifting far into Hunland, I started the homeward journey. It was amusing as they came after me like bees, firing wildly (they must have fired 4,000 rounds in all and not one ever hit my machine) and they were able to keep up with me as I had to keep turning to upset their aim. Whenever one became troublesome I turned on him, and away they would all go like rabbits.... My total is now 36[*], making me second to Guynemer, the Frenchman, and third to Richthofen, the German, and second in record to any Englishman, Ball having 43.[31]

According to his logbook, that was his only flight on the 29th; a nasty little storm brewed up in the early afternoon to keep the whole

---

[*] Apparently he was not counting his two balloons on this occasion.

squadron on the ground. But Arthur Bishop has a different tale to tell, one never mentioned in *Winged Warfare*, one which he presumably got from a letter that is not in the DHH collection or from his father by word of mouth. Arthur writes that, after the storm was over, Billy took off alone and encountered two enemy two-seaters over Monchy. While stalking them, his engine was hit by anti-aircraft fire and "immediately his engine spluttered and slowed."

> He pushed the throttle cautiously open … and suddenly flames enveloped the plane's nose and were blown back towards the cockpit. The smoke and heat choked Bishop.… The flames licked at the fabric of the lower wing and charred pieces tore off.… One of the struts was on fire. When it burned through, the wing would collapse and drop the plane like a stone.… He ducked his head as flames swept around the cockpit; with a violent shudder the plane stopped in mid-air, turned on its side, and crashed into the poplars.… What remained of his SE 5 was a mangled mass of fabric and wire dangling between two tall poplars.…
>
> The amazing fact was that Bishop did not receive so much as a scratch or the trace of a burn.… Cochrane-Patrick [sic] sent him to Amiens for two days' rest.… When he returned to Filescamp Farm his SE 5 was, incredibly, ready to fly.[32]

This preposterous story is reiterated, even more dramatically, by McCaffrey. At least Arthur has admitted to "poetic licence" — fairy stories might be more accurate — but McCaffrey has no such excuse. Very occasionally, a pilot whose aircraft had been set on fire

Lieutenant Colonel Ibbotson Leonard and officers of the 7th Canadian Mounted Rifles in April 1915. Twenty-year-old Lieutenant William Avery "Billy" Bishop is on the left of the rear row — apparently the only officer in the regiment without a moustache!

Lieutenant W. M. "Willie" Fry, MC, Bishop's deputy flight commander in 60 Squadron, who questioned his leader's record and was posted to the Home Establishment for his pains.

Major James McCudden, VC, DSO and Bar, MC and Bar, who had joined the RFC as a private soldier in 1913. Twenty-one of his fifty-seven credited victories fell within the Allied lines. He died in a flying accident in July 1918.

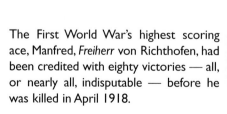

An Allied fighter — either a Nieuport or SPAD — goes down in flames. This was a common sight during "Bloody April" in the spring of 1917 and, in an era before parachutes, a particularly unpleasant way to die.

The First World War's highest scoring ace, Manfred, *Freiherr* von Richthofen, had been credited with eighty victories — all, or nearly all, indisputable — before he was killed in April 1918.

Second Lieutenant (later Captain, DSO and Bar, MC) Albert Ball, 13 Squadron, who would become the RFC's leading ace before his May 1917 death and posthumous VC.

Author's collection

Author's collection

Captain (later Major) Edward "Mick" Mannock, DSO and Bar, MC and Bar, whose official score of fifty — according to his posthumous VC citation — would be inflated to seventy-three by post-war admirers. Mannock was certainly the outstanding British patrol leader of the war.

Author's collection

Ball's grave, with cross erected and a simple epitaph promulgated by the enemy.

Hauptmann Oswald Boelcke, who raised the tactics of air fighting to a new level before his death in an air-to-air collision with one of his own pilots in October 1916.

Author's collection

A 1917 picture of the pilots of *Jasta* 11, with Manfred von Richthofen sitting in the cockpit of an Albatros D-III and his brother Lothar sitting cross-legged on the ground.

Major A.J.L. "Jack" Scott, MC, the crippled officer who commanded 60 Squadron in the spring and early summer of 1917, to whom Bishop owed so much and who encouraged Bishop's exaggerations.

Captain Keith Caldwell, MC (and later DFC), 60 Squadron's senior flight commander, was another who doubted Bishop's claims.

Bishop in the cockpit of his Nieuport 17. The Lewis gun is pulled down, as was required to change the magazine.

A studio portrait of Bishop wearing the "glorious flying coat" given him by Lady St. Helier.

Bishop, who was fond of animals, clutching his large — and "smelly" — pet, "Nigger."

in the air might be lucky enough to put the fire out by diving or side-slipping steeply, but it is inconceivable that a burning plane that had crashed into trees would not burn up immediately and completely, since the seasoned wooden frame and "doped" fabric with which it was covered were both highly flammable. However, the story is easily disproved without resorting to logic, for the morning flight in company with Caldwell and Gunner (also reported by Arthur) makes the date irrefutable, and Bishop's logbook establishes that he never flew at all that afternoon or evening.

Indeed, he did not fly for the next six days, which would account for the local leave and allow time for the aircraft to be repaired had the story been true; but a letter to Margaret Burden, dated 2 August, reported that "the last five days have been dud and no flying." He expanded on that two days later. "For seven days it has rained, and we haven't caught a glimpse of the sun. I am dying to fly and it is impossible." No mention of any flaming crash. Arthur Bishop, however, ends by quoting a different letter to Margaret — one written a month earlier and already cited in this chapter — to explain the effect of his narrow escape on Bishop *père*. "I don't suppose my nerves will last more than three months [more] out here. They are getting shaky now."

It seems superfluous to add that it would have been virtually impossible to repair a machine that had undergone such a trial by fire. If the crash had really happened, Bishop would have been flying a differently numbered aircraft from that time on, but his logbook makes it clear that he continued to fly the same machine for as long as he was with the squadron.

His 4 August letter to Margaret also reported that "I have just learned the general has put me in for another DSO, apart from the VC thing altogether." At that time, Higgins would have had no indication that his VC recommendation had been approved and was about to be promulgated. He could reasonably assume, however, that his protégé would, at a minimum, get a Bar to his DSO, and he must have intended this latest recommendation to bring Bishop a second Bar if the worst came to the worst. The citation was written, according to internal evidence (i.e., the number of victories mentioned) in mid-August, but Bishop apparently knew of it at least ten days earlier. It focused again on his morale-building value to the RFC, recording that, "His consistent gallantry and great fearlessness have set a magnificent example to the pilots of his squadron ... on all occasions displaying a fighting spirit and determination to get to close quarters with his opponents which have earned the admiration of all in contact with him."[33]

Whether his claims were having the hoped-for effect on his fellow airmen seems doubtful, even in his own squadron. Despite his 45 claims from 108 alleged fights, the next most combative pilot in the unit, Molesworth (who had been with the squadron longer than anyone), had accounted for just 4-1/2 in the course of 58 fights, while Caldwell (who had joined two weeks after Bishop) had claimed 4 in 56 fights.[34]

VC submissions were supposed to be confidential, and usually were, but not surprisingly in this case the media had picked up on Bishop's recommendation. No doubt Lady St. Helier and Major Scott (now recuperating from his wound in England) would have played some part in that. As early as mid-June the Toronto *Globe*, for one, had carried a story under the headline "Huns Crushed in Air Battles" that recounted how "One young British pilot* who bids fair soon to rival the record made by the late Captain Ball, emulat-

---

* Canadian citizenship had not yet been invented. All Canadians were British citizens.

ed the latter a few days ago by deliberately 'sitting' over a German aerodrome some twenty miles within the enemy line and smashing, one by one, four machines which came up to attack him."[35]

Now, however, someone had been talking out of turn, and the newspapers had put a name to the story and were proclaiming the imminence of a VC. "How awfully awkward, such a thing getting into the paper when it just isn't so," Bishop wrote to Margaret on 2 August.[36] "There is no news of it yet. They keep such things in 'obeyance' [sic] a long time, but everyone tells me it is sure to come." Two days later, he was responding to a letter from his father which had included "extraordinary accounts of my prowess & clippings, etc., in it.... The nasty part is, cuttings have appeared in English papers, saying VC, etc., too.... I do wish this thing hadn't leaked out.... I get letters by the dozens from people in England I never heard of, telling me the most absurd rot, of what a wonderful hero I be." In all likelihood, however, he just loved the attention.

Bishop claimed two more victims on 5 August, while he was leading Molesworth and Horn against eight enemy machines — presumably scouts, since two-seaters and their escorts rarely flew in such numbers — at a height of 12,000 feet. "I picked out the leader myself, and fired on him," he told his sister.

> In a moment he burst into flames and fell like a great white ball of fire. I then fought [another] one & Moley and Horn got one, and I got another. That left five. Moley & Horn had gun jams and left, and I fought merrily for 15 minutes, my guns also stopping. I would dash for the lines, the Huns after me. I'd turn when they started firing & present them

with a cross-shot (practically impossible) then bluff them that I was about to open fire. They would scatter, and I would turn or loop and dash for the lines again, making another 400 yards.[37]

What was he doing, looping in combat — or was he just using a figure of speech in writing to a young girl who would have little understanding of aerial fighting? More intriguingly, how did it happen that three pilots, each with one belt-fed and one magazine-fed gun, should all get stoppages of both weapons? It would seem that Molesworth and Horn should have seen the first of his victims fall, since a "great white ball of fire" (he told Margaret that "I've never seen such a sight, just a huge mass of flames") would surely have been enough to attract their momentary attention, even in the heat of battle. But neither of them is cited as a witness in his combat report.

> The next day I met the same crowd again, three of them under some clouds. I attacked and in a moment suspected a trap so I zoomed up thro' the clouds just in time to see three more dive thro'. I dived in pursuit and got one. It crashed straight into the ground. I then escaped. These new machines are priceless and I'll do a lot on them, I know.[38]

His forty-second successful claim came on 9 August, while flying alone again, north of Vitry, after an unsuccessful engagement with a solitary enemy.

> At 9.00 am ... I saw a 2-seater this side of the line. I climbed up to him and when a mile from him he

put his nose down & re-crossed the line. I followed
and overhauled him. The observer was firing all the
time & I kept under his tail plane, waiting for his
gun to jam or run out of ammunition. I got within
75 yds of him and opened fire. He fell completely
out of control and finally spun and crashed into a
field N[orth] of Ecourt St. Quentin.[39]

The next day, 10 August 1917, ambition and expectation became
reality. "This afternoon a message came for me to ring up General
Trenchard, which I did, and he said he wanted to be the first to congratulate me on getting the VC. So it is added to my collection of ribbons. The three [VC, DSO and MC] look very swanky, really, and I
try hard not to push my chest out any more than I can help."[40] On the
12th, after a wild celebration in the mess the night before, he lunched
with Trenchard, who told him that he would not be returning to
France after his forthcoming leave, scheduled to begin in a week's
time. The War Office was reluctant to risk losing this new hero before
it had extracted the maximum propaganda advantage from him, and
he would be posted to be chief instructor at a new school for fighter
pilots that the RFC was forming in England.[41]

He needed one more victim to match Ball's total, two to make
him the Empire's "ace of aces." After two uneventful sorties that
evening, one flown in company and one alone, the next day he
claimed the requisite two victories, "shot down in flames" south of
Douai, while flying (according to his logbook) a "DOP" — which
implies he was not alone. A letter to Margaret, however, makes no
mention of anyone being with him.

I had a great scrap last night with three Huns. I had
just climbed through some clouds and three of the

blighters dived on me. I went head on for the first one, firing both guns. He lost his nerve and I filled him with lead. He fell in flames. I then fought the other two and sent one of them down in flames, while the other escaped.[42]

After a solo flight in "stormy" weather on the 14th, he reported that he saw three enemy aircraft but was unable to engage them. The next day, however, flying in company again, he claimed one foe driven down "completely out of control" — no witnesses! — and on the 16th, flying alone, two more that "crashed" for his forty-sixth and forty-seventh victims. He had now surpassed Ball by three, and did not fly at all on his last two days in France. On Sunday, 19 August 1917, he set off back to England and public adulation. In Canada, the newspapers were full of him and his feats. He was an imperial and national hero who had surely proven himself worthy of an Eaton heiress. When would he come home to a hero's welcome?

CHAPTER 6

A Statistical Interlude

As far as his combat reports show, only three and a half or four of
Bishop's claimed forty-seven victories while he was with 60
Squadron were witnessed. Three are demonstrably false, eleven are
highly suspect on the basis of Bishop's own descriptions of the fights as
given in his combat reports or logbook, and one other — that which
he originally "shared" with Fry — is controversial to say the least.

When a First World War fighter pilot claimed a victim, it was
customary, but obviously not obligatory, for eyewitnesses to be identified on the combat report as part of the authentication process.
Such was the case with Bishop's first two victims, observed by antiaircraft gunners in both cases, as well as a fellow pilot in the second.

Were there good reasons for the lack of witnesses in so many of
Bishop's reports? Sometimes, apparently yes. When he identified loca-
tions where his alleged victories had occurred (which was not that
often), they often put him deep in German airspace, thus eliminating
the possibility of sympathetic witnesses on the ground. When he was
hunting alone, as he so often was, it would be exceptional for the fall
of an adversary to be seen by a fellow airman or airmen flying in his

vicinity by chance. There were occasions when, as with those first two victories, his achievement should have been visible to ground-based observers in the British front line (for example, that of 17 July 1917, when he claimed his thirty-fourth victory "in flames" while flying alone close to the front in the vicinity of Havrincourt). There was no obligation on them to report it, however, and no clear official chain of communication through which to make such a report.

As for those times when he was flying in company, Bishop's comrades would often have found more important things to concern themselves with than tracking the fate of their leader's erstwhile opponents. Still, other fighter pilots on the Western Front, such as Raymond Collishaw or Edward Mannock — Bishop's posthumous rival for the scoring crown — seem to have found witnesses on most occasions. Of course, there is always the theoretical possibility that Bishop's colleagues did see his opponents fall and that, after those first two victories, Bishop did not bother to record their evidence since it was clear to him that his superiors would support all his claims, witnessed or not. But that seems unlikely. If he had evidence, it would have been sensible to offer it. After all, he could never be absolutely sure that his claims would be unquestioningly accepted — particularly, for example, when Caldwell was acting squadron commander or when Kennedy-Cochran-Patrick took over command of the squadron from Scott.

Aircraft allegedly "driven down out of control" were always doubtful triumphs in a category not recognized by either the French or Germans. One obvious way for an opponent to escape further combat was to spin down deliberately, almost to ground level, and then slink away. With other hostile aircraft in the vicinity (or even without them), an opponent would usually be unwilling to confirm his success by sacrificing height to follow his apparent victim down. A machine often a mile below, and sometimes two or more, would have been extremely difficult to follow visually, requiring total concentration on the part of the onlooker at a time and place where concentration on anything but personal survival was likely to prove fatal.

Kite balloons destroyed at height would probably be noticed and recorded by friendly ground observers, since the fireball that resulted when the gasbag's hydrogen contents ignited would be apparent at some considerable distance. As for those that merely "smoked," they were unlikely to be victories. Damaged, no doubt, but not destroyed. Both of Bishop's claimed balloons were smokers, allegedly destroyed on or near to the ground.

Finally, woefully incomplete records make it impractical to confirm or deny most of his claims from German sources.

Thus there can be no "hard" analysis of most of Bishop's assertions on an individual basis. Still, it is possible to look at them from a statistical perspective. Let us begin with a table illustrating Bishop's first month at the front, while he was adjusting to this new environment and discovering the values and attitudes of his superiors, particularly his commanding officer and wing commander.

Date	Sortie Number	Claim in Combat Report or Logbook	Location	Patrol or Alone	Official Dispostition	Victory No.	Witness
17/3/17	1	No enemy reported	Bapaume/Vimy	Patrol			
24/3/17	2	No enemy reported	Cambrai	Patrol			
"	3	No enemy reported	Douai	Patrol			
25/3/17	4	No enemy reported	?	Patrol			
"	5	No enemy reported	?	Patrol			
"	6	E/A "crashed"	Arras	Patrol	Destroyed	1	Yes
28/3/17	7	No enemy reported	?	Patrol			
30/3/17	8	1 indecisive combat	Arras/Douai	Patrol			
31/3/17	9	E/A "crashed"	NE of Arras	Patrol	Destroyed	2	Yes
1/4/17	10	No enemy reported	?	Patrol			
2/4/17	11	Enemy seen — not engaged	?	Alone			
"	12	No enemy reported	?	Patrol			
3/4/17	13	No enemy reported	?	Patrol			
4/4/17	14	No enemy reported	?	Patrol			
5/4/17	15	No enemy reported	?	Patrol			
"	16	No enemy reported	Arras	Alone			
6/4/17	17	2 indecisive combats	Vitry-en-Artois	Alone			
7/4/17	18	E/A "dived away steeply"	Arras	Alone	DDOOC*	3	No

Date	No.	Report	Location		Disposition		
"	"	Balloon "smoked" on ground	Vis-en-Artois	Alone	Destroyed*	4	No
"	19	No enemy reported	?	Alone			
8/4/17	20	"Nose dive 500 ft from ground"	Vitry	Patrol	Destroyed*	5	No
"	"	"Nose well down"	NE of Arras	Patrol	DDOOC*	6	No
"	"	"Spinning nose dive"	"	Patrol	DDOOC*	7	No
"	21	Enemy seen — not engaged	?	Alone			
10/4/17	22	No enemy reported	E of Monchy	Alone			
11/4/17	23	1 indecisive combat	E of Arras	Patrol			
12/4/17	24	No enemy reported	?	Patrol			
13/4/17	25	No enemy reported	?	Alone			
"	26	No enemy reported	?	Patrol			
"	27	No enemy reported	?	Patrol			
"	28	No enemy reported	?	Patrol			
14/4/17	29	No enemy reported	?	Alone			
"	30	Enemy seen — not engaged	?	Patrol			
"	31	Enemy seen — not engaged	?	Alone			
"	32	No enemy reported	?	Alone			

*Official disposition not justified in light of Bishop's combat reports.

His first two victories were certainly genuine, but the remaining five with which he was credited, and upon which he appears to have reported honestly, were all unwarranted on the basis of his own descriptions of the results of his fights.

Of thirty-two sorties, twenty-two were flown as part of a patrol, and on fifteen of them no hostile aircraft were seen, while on two others enemies were seen but not actually encountered. When fighting in company, there were seven engagements (two in the course of one sortie, and three on another occasion) resulting in five credited victories, three of which were very doubtful indeed. Even taken at face value, that works out to one victory for every 1.4 engagements, which was the sort of phenomenal result one would hardly expect even from an experienced leader, with excellent backup, flying a technologically superior machine. The Red Baron at his peak would have been proud of such results.

Ten sorties were flown alone, with no adversaries seen on six of them and adversaries seen, but not engaged, on one. Three sorties included combats, and they brought him two more (doubtful) victories, or one for every 1.5 engagements. Had all his credited victories been valid, those would have been astounding results for a veteran ace, never mind a novice, given the normal nature of aerial combat in 1917.

During the next five weeks of flying (not including two weeks' leave in England), Bishop's claims became slightly more reasonable, though the figures are still much higher than one might expect, even allowing for his acquisition of the "souped-up" Nieuport 17, which may have enabled him to become rather more venturesome without increasing the awesome risks he ran when he flew alone. Note that he was now flying as many as *ten* sorties *in two days* (22–23 May) — most fighter pilots only flew that many in a week — and he allegedly engaged enemy aircraft on six of them.

Date	Sortie Number	Claim in Combat Report or Logbook	Location	Patrol or Alone	Official Dispostition	Victory No.	Witness
20/4/17	33	No enemy reported	?	Alone			
"	34	No enemy reported	?	Patrol			
"	35	"Flames were visible"	Biache St, Vaast	Alone	Destroyed	8	No
21/4/17	36	No enemy reported	?	Patrol			
"	37	No enemy reported	?	Patrol			
"	38	No enemy reported	?	Alone			
22/4/17	39	"Apparently out of control"	Vis-en-Artois	Patrol	DDOOC*	9	No
"	40	1 indecisive combat	?	Alone			
"	41	3 indecisive combats	Crosilles/Bailleul	Alone			
"	42	No enemy reported	?	Patrol			
"	43	No enemy reported	?	Patrol			
23/4/17	44	Enemy seen — not engaged	E of Monchy	Alone			
"	45	No enemy reported	?	Patrol			
"	46	A/c. landed — shot at crew on ground	Vitry	Alone	DDOOC*	10	No
"	"	"Saw him crash"	E of Vitry	Alone	Destroyed	11	No
"	47	Reconnaissance	Vis-en-Artois	Alone			
"	48	1 indecisive combat	Croisilles	Alone			
24/4/17	49	Indecisive on balloon	?	Alone			
25/4/17	50	Enemy seen — not engaged	?	Patrol			
"	51	No enemy reported	?	Patrol			
26/4/17	52	Enemy seen — not engaged	?	Alone			
"	53	No enemy reported	?	Patrol			
27/4/17	54	No enemy reported	?	Patrol			
"	55	"Saw balloon smoking"	W of Vitry	Alone	Destroyed*	12	No

Date	Sortie Number	Claim in Combat Report or Logbook	Location	Patrol or Alone	Official Disposition	Victory No.	Witness
"	56	Indecisive on balloon	Vitry	Alone			
28/4/17	57	Enemy seen — not engaged	?	Patrol			
"	58	Enemy seen — not engaged	?	Alone			
"	59	1 indecisive combat	Bois-du-Sart	Patrol			
29/4/17	60	Enemy seen — not engaged	?	Alone			
"	61	"Burst into flames"	E of Epinoy	Patrol	Destroyed	13	No
"	62	2 indecisive combats	E of Epinoy	Patrol			
30/4/17	63	2 indecisive combats	N and S of Lens	Patrol			
"	64	"In a spin … 1,000 ft from ground"	S of Lens	Alone	Destroyed* 1	4	No
"	65	4 indecisive combats	Lens/Monchy/Wancourt	Alone			
"	66	1 indecisive combat	E of Lens	Patrol			
1/5/17	67	Enemy seen — not engaged	?	Patrol			
"	68	Enemy seen — not engaged	?	Patrol			
"	69	Enemy seen — not engaged	?	Patrol			
2/5/17	70	E/A "crashed"	S of Henin-Liétard	Patrol	Destroyed	15	No
"	71	"Spinning nose dive"	S of Henin-Liétard	Patrol	DDOOC	16	No
"	72	4 indecisive combats	Lens/Monchy/Pelves	Alone			
"	73	3 indecisive combats	Lens/Monchy/Pelves	Alone			
3/5/17	74	2 indecisive combats	S of Vis-en-Artois	Patrol			
"	75	No enemy reported	?	Patrol			
"	76	1 indecisive combat	?	Patrol			
4/5/17	77	"We saw him crash"	Brebières-Vitry	Patrol	Destroyed†	17	Yes/No

Date	No.		Location				
5/5/17	78	Enemy seen — not engaged	?	Alone			
"	79	Enemy seen — not engaged	?	Patrol			
"	80	No enemy reported	?	Patrol			
"	81	Enemy seen — not engaged	?	Patrol			
7/5/17	82	Enemy seen — not engaged	?	Alone			
"	83	"In a spin" & smoking	Henin-Liétard	Alone	DDOOC*	18	No
"	84	"Only partly under control"	S of Brebières	Patrol	DDOOC*	19	No
"	85	1 indecisive combat	S of Brebières	Patrol			
8/5/17	86	No enemy reported	?	Patrol			
25/5/17	87	No enemy reported	?	Alone			
"	88	Enemy seen — not engaged	?	Alone			
"	89	No enemy reported	?	Alone			
26/5/17	90	1 indecisive combat	S of Vitry	Patrol			
"	91	"Completely out of control"	Izel-les-Esquerchin	Alone	DDOOC	20	No
"	92	1 indecisive combat	Lens	Alone			
27/5/17	93	E/A "crashed"	Dourgies	Alone	Destroyed	21	No
"	94	1 indecisive combat	E of Monchy	Patrol			
"	95	3 indecisive combats	E of Lens/Lens/Vimy	Alone			
"	96	Enemy seen — not engaged	?	Alone			
28/5/17	97	Enemy seen — not engaged	?	Alone			
"	98	Enemy seen — not engaged	?	Alone			
"	99	Enemy seen — not engaged	?	Patrol			
30/5/17	100	1 indecisive combat	?	Patrol			
31/5/17	101	"Crashed"	Near Epinoy	Alone	Destroyed	22	No

*Official disposition not justified in light of Bishop's combat reports.
†Bizarre and doubtful on the basis of Fry's later reminiscences.

The result of one sortie, Number 77, in which he allegedly shared his seventeenth victory with Willie Fry, has been included in these calculations despite its extremely uncertain and contradictory nature which might well justify omitting it entirely.

Thus, of sixty-nine sorties, the thirty-six that were flown in company included twelve on which no opponents were seen and eight on which foes were seen but no engagement occurred. There were 18 fights and Bishop was credited with seven victories, three again being doubtful according to his own reports and one being that shared with Fry. Including these latter four, that works out to one victory in 2.6 fights, compared to the one in 1.4 he claimed during his first month at the front — a curious inversion from what one might anticipate. A pilot would be expected to get better with experience and achieve a proportionally higher success rate, not a lower one.

The same peculiarity marked his other operational sorties. No enemy aircraft were seen on four of thirty-three solitary flights, while the enemy was seen but not engaged on ten, and thirty fights brought nine alleged victories, or just one in every 3.3 combats — compared with one in every 1.5 during the previous month. There was no obvious tactical or technological reason why this should be so. Had the German airmen suddenly become much more skilful, or was Bishop losing some previous magical touch?

The next seven weeks included the VC–winning raid of 2 June — with its three demonstrably false claims, but since they were accepted as victories by his superiors, they are counted as such in this summary.

Date	Sortie Number	Claim in Combat Report or Logbook	Location	Patrol or Alone	Official Dispostition	Victory No.	Witness
1/6/17	102	1 indecisive combat	Pelves	Patrol			
"	103	Enemy seen — not engaged	?	Alone			
"	104	Enemy seen — not engaged	?	Alone			
"	105	Enemy seen — not engaged	?	Patrol			
2/6/17	106	E/A "crashed"	?	Alone	Destroyed*	23	No
"	"	" "	?	Alone	Destroyed*	24	No
"	"	" "	?	Alone	Destroyed*	25	No
3/6/17	107	Enemy seen — not engaged	?	Patrol			
"	108	Enemy seen — not engaged	?	Alone			
"	109	Enemy seen — not engaged	?	Alone			
4/6/17	110	Enemy seen — not engaged	?	Alone			
"	111	2 indecisive combats	Etaing/Neuvireuil	Patrol			
6/6/17	112	No enemy reported	?	Alone			
"	113	No enemy reported	?	Alone			
7/6/17	114	Enemy seen — not engaged	?	Alone			
"	115	Enemy seen — not engaged	?	Patrol			
8/6/17	116	"Straight into the ground"	N of Lille	Alone	Destroyed	26	No
"	117	3 indecisive combats	NE of Lens/ SW of Lille	Alone			

Date	Sortie Number	Claim in Combat Report or Logbook	Location	Patrol or Alone	Official Dispostition	Victory No.	Witness
9/6/17	118	No enemy reported	?	Alone			
12/6/17	119	Enemy seen — not engaged	?	Alone			
"	120	No enemy reported	?	Alone			
13/6/17	121	Enemy seen — not engaged	?	Patrol			
"	122	Enemy seen — not engaged	?	Patrol			
15/6/17	123	1 Indecisive combat	Boiry Notre-Dame	Patrol			
"	124	Enemy seen — not engaged	E of Vitry	Patrol			
"	125	1 Indecisive combat	S of Vitry	Patrol			
22/6/17	126	1 Indecisive combat	S of Brebières	Patrol			
24/6/17	127	Enemy seen — not engaged	?	Patrol			
"	128	1 Indecisive combat	SW of Douai	Alone			
"	129	"He burst into flames"	N of Beaumont	Alone	Destroyed	27	No
"	130	No enemy reported	?	Alone			
25/6/17	131	"Completely out of control"	Dury	Patrol	DDOOC	28	No
"	132	No enemy reported	?	Alone			
26/6/17	133	"He burst into flames"	Annay	Alone	Destroyed	29	No
"	"	"Went down out of control"	Annay	Alone	DDOOC	30	No
"	134	1 Indecisive combat	?	Alone			
"	135	No enemy reported	?	Alone			

Date	No.	Combat	Location		Disposition		
27/6/17	136	2 Indecisive combats	?	Alone			
"	137	3 Indecisive combats	Near Henin-Liétard	Alone			
28/6/17	138	"Apparently about to land" (CR) or "shot down … OOC" (logbook)	Drocourt-La Bassée	Alone	DDOOC†	31	No
"	139	No enemy reported	?	Patrol			
1/7/17	140	Enemy seen — not engaged	?	Patrol			
"	141	Enemy seen — not engaged	?	Alone			
"	142	2 Indecisive combats	?	Patrol			
7/7/17	143	Enemy seen — not engaged	?	Patrol			
"	144	1 Indecisive combat	NE of Quéant	Patrol			
10/7/17	145	"Still spinning" at 10,000 ft	Quiéry-la-Motte	Patrol	DDOOC†	32	No
"	146	1 Indecisive combat	?	Patrol			

*Demonstrably false on the basis of German records.
†Official disposition not justified in light of Bishop's combat reports.

These seven weeks brought twenty sorties flown in company. On only one of them was no enemy seen; on another ten, the enemy was seen but not engaged. Bishop was involved in twelve fights, which resulted in two claims (one of which was *very* doubtful based on the description in his combat report), or one victory in six combats. While flying alone, his twenty-four sorties included seven on which no enemy was seen and six on which enemies were seen but not engaged. Eighteen fights resulted in eight confirmed claims (including three which we know to have been false, and a fourth "shot down" according to his logbook, but "forced to land" according to his combat report), for a ratio of one victory in every 2.25 sorties. Although he had now been credited with thirty-two victories, his ratio of success to fights was still dropping toward a somewhat more realistic figure.

It quickly became obvious that Scott's successor, Kennedy-Cochran-Patrick — with Pretyman, Higgins and even Trenchard looking over his shoulder — was not about to clamp down on Bishop's expanding claims, which can only be partially explained or justified by his acquisition of a new and superior machine, an SE 5, in the last week of July.

Date	Sortie Number	Claim in Combat Report or Logbook	Location	Patrol or Alone	Official Dispostition	Victory No.	Witness
11/7/17	147	Enemy seen — not engaged	?	Alone			
12/7/17	148	Enemy seen — not engaged	?	Patrol			
"	149	"Crashed"	Near Vitry	Patrol	Destroyed	33	Yes
"	150	1 indecisive combat	Near Vitry	Alone			
13/7/17	151	1 indecisive combat	Croisilles	Patrol			
15/7/17	152	Enemy seen — not engaged	?	Patrol			
16/7/17	153	No enemy reported	?	Patrol			
17/7/17	154	"In flames"	Havrincourt	Alone	Destroyed	34	No
"	"	Out of control"	Marquion-Quéant	Alone	DDOOC	35	No
20/7/17	155	"Out of control"	SE of Havrincourt	Alone	DDOOC	36	No
"	"	1 indecisive combat	E of Havrincourt	Alone			
21/7/17	156	1 indecisive combat	?	Patrol			
22/7/17	157	Enemy seen — not engaged	?	Patrol			
"	158	Enemy seen — not engaged	?	Patrol			
23/7/17	159	1 indecisive combat	E of Lens	Alone			
"	160	1 indecisive combat	Fampoux	Patrol			
24/7/17	161	Enemy seen — not engaged	?	Patrol			
27/7/17	162	Enemy seen — not engaged	?	Patrol			
"	163	1 indecisive combat	Arleux	Patrol			
"	164	Enemy seen — not engaged	?	Patrol			
28/7/17	165	No enemy reported	?	Alone			
"	166	"He burst into flames"	Phalempin	Alone	Destroyed	37	No
"	167	1 indecisive combat	Phalempin	Alone			

Date	Sortie Number	Claim in Combat Report or Logbook	Location	Patrol or Alone	Official Disposition	Victory No.	Witness
29/7/17	168	"Completely out of control"	Beaumont	Alone	DDOOC	38	No
5/8/17	169	"Burst into flames"	N of Hendecourt	Patrol	Destroyed	39	No
"	"	"Completely out of control"	N of Hendecourt	Patrol	DDOOC	40	No
6/8/17	170	No enemy reported	?	Alone			
"	171	"Crashed"	Brebières	Patrol	Destroyed	41	No
8/8/17	172	No enemy reported	?	Alone			
9/8/17	173	"Spun and crashed"	Escourt St. Quentin	Alone	Destroyed	42	No
"	174	1 indecisive combat	N of Vitry-en-Artois	Alone			
"	175	1 indecisive combat	?	Patrol			
11/8/17	176	No enemy reported	?	Patrol			
"	177	No enemy reported	?	Patrol			
12/8/17	178	No enemy reported	?	Alone			
"	179	Enemy seen — not engaged	?	Patrol			
13/8/17	180	"Shot down in flames"	S of Douai	Patrol	Destroyed	43	No
"	"	"Shot down in flames"	S of Douai	Patrol	Destroyed	44	No
14/8/17	181	Enemy seen — not engaged	?	Alone			
15/8/17	182	"Completely out of control"	NE of Henin-Liétard	Patrol	DDOOC	45	No
16/8/17	183	"Crashed — planes fell off"	Harnes	Alone	Destroyed	46	No
"	184	"Spun in and crashed"	Carvin	Alone	Destroyed	47	No

Bishop had learned his lessons well. The style adopted in his combat reports no longer allows for any doubt, nor does it require interpretation by his superiors to establish success; now his adversaries either "crash," "burst into flames" or are driven down "*completely* out of control.*" Figures for sorties flown in company remain believable — twenty-one sorties, on three of which no enemy was seen, and eight when the enemy was seen but not engaged. In twelve fights he claimed six victories (one of which was witnessed), or one in every two engagements. In seventeen solitary sorties, he did not see any enemies on four occasions and twice he reported seeing but not engaging them, while in the course of thirteen fights he claimed to have shot down eight, or one in every 1.6.

While flying in company, his overall ratio of fights to sorties while with 60 Squadron was one fight in every 2.3 sorties; of victories to fights, one in every 2.7; and of victories to sorties, one in 10.9. Flying alone, his ratio of fights to sorties was one in 1.3; of victories to fights, one in 2.4; and of victories to sorties, one in 3.1.

These figures may not seem extreme when examined from the comfort of an armchair eighty-odd years after the event, but those few scout pilots who lived long enough commonly flew hundreds of sorties in accumulating less than a dozen victories. Willie Fry, for example, one of the lucky ones, flew nearly four hundred sorties in some fourteen months of operational flying, became a flight commander, and won a well-deserved MC in the course of accounting for eleven enemy machines — or one victory in every 34.6 sorties.[1] With 60 Squadron, Bishop racked up 47 alleged victories in the course of 184 sorties flown over four-and-a- half months, or one victory in every 3.9 sorties!

And with Bishop, still more amazing things were to come.

CHAPTER 7

"I Have Never Been So Furious in My Life"

Writing to Bishop's mother about the forthcoming investiture, Lady St. Helier reported that Princess Marie Louise had told her that the King was looking forward to presenting Billy with a VC, DSO and MC all at once — "something he had never yet done for anyone" — and most particularly because "he [the King] has heard so very much about him from the Princess."[1] On 29 August, Bishop "received my medals from the King.... Oh darling, it was too awful for words, for fifteen minutes the old boy talked to me in front of a huge crowd. I nearly died."[2] If the investiture had been held a week later, the monarch could have presented him with another DSO as well, for Bishop learned on 5 September that he had been awarded a Bar! The newspapers had already burst into paeans of praise, he was photographed by society photographers, the Canadian government commissioned a marble bust of his handsome head and shoulders and his schedule of public appearances and social commitments became ever more arduous — until St. Helier, taking pity on him, arranged a country holiday that involved visits to the homes of several of her aristocratic friends.

When he returned to London, he learned that he had been promoted to the rank of major, but that construction of the airfield where the new gunnery school was scheduled to be set up was not going well. It would be months before the school would be ready to accept instructors, never mind pupils, and so he had time on his hands. Sir Richard Turner, like Bishop a VC winner (his from the Boer War), set in motion arrangements for another home leave. The price to be paid would be a series of public relations appearances, in the United States as well as Canada, in which he would make speeches to raise money and enthusiasm for the war. The Canadian press, fuelled by Beaverbrook's propaganda machine, was already worshipping at the Bishop shrine. "The Young Hero," "Famous Canadian Aviator" and "Greatest Air Fighter" were just three headlines among many.

He landed in Canada on 25 September 1917 and found himself praised in Parliament and at the centre of patriotic rallies in Montreal, Kingston, Ottawa and Toronto — and, of course, in Owen Sound, where there was a civic reception. The Burdens could hardly object to their daughter marrying a national hero — indeed, it would seem they had come to accept the idea during his earlier leave, when he and Margaret had become engaged. On 17 October, he married her in a Toronto ceremony attended by the cream of Canadian society. The honeymoon, comfortable but not luxurious, took them to the Catskill Mountains, south of Albany, New York.

His leave ended on 1 November, and as of that date he was attached to the British War Mission in Washington, which was providing American industry with much-needed technical know-how on military matters. But Bishop was not there for his technical wizardry, which was probably close to zero; his business was to raise money — and enthusiasm — with a riot of patriotic speeches. As we have noted, he was also finding time to write *Winged Warfare*. Just over two months later, on 12 January 1918 — with the manuscript presumably in the hands of his publisher — he embarked for England once again. This time, Margaret — Mrs. Bishop — came with him.

The gunnery school project had been abandoned for the moment, and in February 1918 he was assigned to command a new fighter squadron, Number 85, which was preparing to go to France. It had been formed at Upavon in August 1917, but had made only limited progress; a start had been made in equipping it with the new Sopwith Dolphin fighter, but those machines were still in short supply. Bishop probably pushed hard for this appointment, perhaps using Lady St. Helier to further his interests with her powerful friends. His competitive streak must have been stimulated by news of James McCudden's forty-seventh victory on 2 February, and his forty-eighth two weeks later, which put him ahead of Bishop as the top-scoring British pilot.* To be turned loose on the Western Front in a Dolphin, "the best operational fighter of its period,"³ with its top speed of close to 140 mph at ground level (nearly 130 mph at 10,000 feet) and two Vickers guns, might give him the opportunity to earn a Bar to his VC.**

He had tested a prototype Dolphin in France nine months earlier.

> *View* — The view is exceptionally good, the pilot
> being able to see everything in front and behind
> him, as well as below him in front. He also has a
> good view above behind [sic].

---

* These claims, and subsequent ones in this chapter, are taken from Shores, Franks and Guest, *Above the Trenches*.

** Lieut. A. Martin-Leake, RAMC, had been awarded the first such Bar on 20 February 1915, after winning the VC during the South African War. Another medical officer, Capt. Noel Chavasse, had won his VC in October 1916 and added a posthumous Bar in August 1917. The only other man ever to wear the VC and Bar was a New Zealand infantryman, Capt. Charles Upham, who won both his during the Second World War.

Handiness — The machine is extraordinarily quick
on turns and very handy.

Guns — The guns are in a position where the pilot
can easily work at them, i.e., when correcting
jams, etc.

Speed — With the engine only giving 2,000 revo-
lutions the speed at 2,000 ft was 106 knots =
122 mph.[4]

In a heavily censored letter to Margaret (the aircraft type, characteristics and performance figures were blacked out) he had reported
that "it is a wonder, a perfect marvel, flies about [censored] miles per
hour and has [censored] guns. Besides which, you can see everything
out of them. By Jove, how I loved it. I wish we had them."[5] Trenchard
had not been quite so impressed, however, and had decided shortly
afterwards that the Royal Aircraft Factory's SE 5a should remain the
RFC's primary fighter for the foreseeable future.[6]

Some pilots were already assigned to the squadron, but after a
refresher flying course at Gosport, Bishop seems to have been given a
free hand in recruiting the remainder. He promptly picked out three
decorated veterans as his flight commanders. One of them was an ex-
colleague from 60 Squadron, Spencer Horn, the son of a wealthy
Australian sheep farmer and businessman, who had more recently
been instructing novice pilots of the U.S. Army's Air Service at Ayr, in
Scotland. Horn brought three of his American students with him:
Elliot Springs, a millionaire industrialist's son; Larry Callahan, from a
banking family that was also well-to-do; and John (Mac) Grider.

With so much money available, the 85 Squadron officers' mess
resembled that of one of the more exclusive British cavalry regiments
— as much an elite social club as a military unit. Grider kept a diary
which, after his death in action and after the war, Springs edited and

published under the title *War Birds: Diary of an Unknown Aviator.* From it we learn that, while 85 Squadron was training in England, champagne flowed like beer and pretty showgirls from London's theatre district were two-a-penny. When the squadron reached France, girls may have been lacking, but the mess parties would still be wondrous things.

Understandably, these three American novices were mightily impressed by their new leader. Grider, recounting their first meeting with him, wrote of how "the whole staff [of the American headquarters in London] nearly lost their eyes staring at us when we strolled out, arm in arm with the great Bishop."[7] His decorations were awesome in themselves, but his roster of society friends was just as impressive. Grider recorded his first meeting with Princess Marie Louise.

> Mrs Bishop had a lady with her and she invited us to tea with them.… The lady with her proved to be very nice and was very much interested in Americans and America. She was the most patriotic person I've met over here because she was always talking about the King. When I told her how much all the Americans liked serving with the British, she said she was glad and she knew the King would be delighted to hear it. That sounded a bit far-fetched to me.… We had a taxi waiting for us and offered to take her back to town [from the airfield at Houndslow] with us as soon as we got dressed. She said she'd rather take a bus and get the air and it would take her right by the palace. I didn't get that either.[8]

Trenchard's decision to make the SE 5a his standard fighter meant that production of the Sopwith Dolphin was further restricted, and now "the factory is short on Dolphins as they have been using all the new ones to replace Spads at the front," wrote Grider. "They have taken our Dolphins and we have to refit with SEs. I'm not sorry to get SEs but I hate the delay." The SE cockpit was a far cry from that of the Nieuport 17, only eighteen months its senior, and gives some idea of how quickly aircraft technology was advancing.

> The cockpit looks like the inside of a locomotive cab. In it is a compass, airspeed indicator, radiator thermometer, oil gauge, compensator, two gun trigger controls, synchronized gear [oil] reservoir handle, hand [fuel] pump, gas tank gauge, two [ignition] switches, pressure control, altimeter, gas pipe, shut off cocks, [fuel and radiator] shutter control, thermometer, two cocking handles for the guns, booster magneto, spare ammunition drums, map case, throttle, joystick and rudder bar. That's enough for any man to say grace over.
>
> It has two guns: one Vickers and one Lewis. The Vickers is mounted on the fuselage in front of your face and fires thru the propeller with a CC gear to keep from hitting it. The Lewis is mounted on the top wing and fires over the top of the propeller. It has two sights: a ring sight and an Aldis telescopic sight. I set both sights and both guns so that they will all converge at a spot two hundred yards in front of the line of flight.[9]

As speeds were increasing, so were the ranges at which pilots set their sights. There were also changes in the tactics and morale of the air war since Bishop had left 60 Squadron. For one thing, the sheer scale of air battles was still increasing. The Germans had led the way, as they had so often done before. On 24 June 1917, *Kronprinz* Rupprecht of Bavaria had announced the formation of *Jagdgeswader* [Fighter Wing] *1* as a self-contained mobile formation dedicated to achieving aerial superiority over specific sectors of front as and when required. It was composed of *Jastas 4, 6, 10* and *11*, and was commanded, of course, by Manfred von Richthofen.

Initially the four *Jastas* flew in separate shifts, but as time passed they began to combine, putting as many as fifty aircraft in the sky at a time. When that happened, *Jagdgeswadern* were formidable fighting forces to which the RFC could respond in only one way — by massing its own squadrons into wing formations. Such concentrations were still unusual in the fall of 1917, but by the spring of 1918 they were rapidly becoming commonplace, with squadrons in a triangular relationship both laterally and vertically.

> ... [F]or example, Sopwith Camels flying at 15,000 feet, front and centre, SE 5as at 16,000–17,000 feet to the right rear, and Bristol Fighters 18,000–19,000 feet, behind the SEs and to the left of the Camels....
>
> Three squadrons, some or all of them carrying bombs, were instructed to fly by widely divergent routes to a specified enemy airfield, ten or fifteen miles east of the lines. At that point they would drop their bombs and then adopt the "stepped triangle" formation and make a wide return sweep from east to west in an attempt to trap any enemy machines between them and the lines.[10]

A major battle took place on 18 March 1918, when such a force was met by more than fifty German fighters, led by von Richthofen and thirty of his *Jagdgeswader 1* pilots. The result was the biggest air mêlée yet seen — large enough, confused enough and profound enough in its implications to be remembered as the Air Battle of Le Cateau. The Germans had the better, more skilled and experienced pilots, and experience won out: the RFC lost eleven machines, the Germans only four.

However, RFC/RNAS morale had begun to improve in the fall of 1917 and was substantially better by 1 April 1918, when the two services were amalgamated into the Royal Air Force. Losses were no longer unbearably high, the Germans appeared to be losing heavily, too, and the death of Voss, followed by that of the great Red Baron in April 1918 (killed either by a bullet from the guns of Canadian Roy Brown's Sopwith Camel, as the RAF trumpeted at the time, or from a Lewis gun on the ground fired by an Australian soldier, as seems more likely), did much to encourage British airmen.

With such massive formations sweeping the skies and squadron-strength patrols becoming commonplace, it might be thought that the day of the lone hunter was totally past. The likelihood of being caught in the face of such overwhelming odds would seem to have transformed solitary sorties into virtual suicide attempts. Not necessarily so, at least not for British pilots; that was because German designers, responding to their airmen's wishes, were emphasizing rate of climb and manoeuvrability in their latest models. Speed was not of primary importance to the Germans, since the RAF was always spoiling for a fight, in accordance with Trenchard's longstanding policy which was now being implemented by his successor, Sir John Salmond. In terms of numbers, the odds had become heavily weighted towards the RAF side and there was no need to chase after the British in order to bring them to battle — they were happy to oblige.

Thus the Albatros D-V/D-Va had a top speed of only 116 mph, compared with the SE 5a's 130-plus and the Dolphin's 140. The

Fokker Dreidekker-I that von Richthofen now favoured was even slower at 103 mph, although the triplane could climb and turn like a cat. The Fokker D-VII, "which was to become the scourge of the skies in the closing months of the 1914–1918 War,"[11] could do no more than 117 mph in level flight. So, the experienced pilot of an SE 5a, were he keeping an extremely careful lookout (as Bishop seems to have excelled at doing) and holding the advantage of height, could probably flee successfully from any number of hostile aircraft he might encounter. The enemy, on the other hand, did not have that option; but other things being equal, he could outmanoeuvre and outfight his opponents, and he usually only chose to fly when other factors — location, weather and numbers — were firmly in his favour.

An SE 5a could not out-dogfight the other leading fighters of the day, one-on-one, as Cecil Lewis discovered when he engaged a Sopwith Dolphin in mock combat.

> ... I was a fairly competent pilot. I could do every stunt then invented with ease and style. I admitted none to be my superior in the handling of an aeroplane. So I confess I dived on the Dolphin with the intention of showing him just how an aeroplane should be flown in a fight, sitting on his tail for a bit, and then, when it was quite obvious I had killed him ten times over, coming up alongside, waving him a gracious goodbye....
>
> But it didn't work out a bit like that. The Dolphin had a better performance than I realised. He was up in a climbing turn and on my tail in a flash. I half rolled out of the way, he was still there. I sat in a tight climbing spiral, he sat in a tighter one. I tried to

climb above him, he climbed faster. Every dodge I had ever learnt I tried on him; but he just sat there on my tail, for all the world as if I had been towing him behind me.[12]

The new German machines, although slower than the SE, were even more nimble than the Dolphin. For SE pilots it made sense to employ a dive-shoot-and-run tactic. They need not run very far before climbing to regain the height advantage (if possible), diving and shooting again. It was, of course, an ideal approach for a situationally aware individual who preferred to fly alone.

On 25 May 1918, 85 Squadron flew to France, to an old RNAS field about two miles south of Dunkirk called Petit Synthe. The coastal sector was a relatively quiet part of the front where new squadrons were commonly posted for their first month on the Western Front to ease them into the routines and dangers of air fighting. Two days later, while his flight commanders were beginning to familiarize their novice pilots with the look of the lines and introducing them to the practice of combat flying, Bishop was off on his own, starting his campaign to overtake McCudden and stay ahead of Mannock, who now had now been credited with forty-one victories. His combat report for 27 May 1918 notes that he was on an "Offensive Patrol," but if his letter to Margaret, written that evening, is to be believed, he was alone. A morning patrol had not met up with any hostile machines. "… [T]his morning I had my guns sighted and a lot of things adjusted, then went out to the lines with Nigger [Horn] and McGregor.… This afternoon at four I went out again, only alone."[13] And, indeed, there is no mention of any other aircraft in his combat report.

While attempting to attack a 2-seater at 13,000 feet over Houthulst Forest, I saw 10 enemy scouts coming from S[outh] E[ast] so climbed towards our lines returning ten minutes later at 17,500 feet. In looking for above 2-seater I suddenly saw another one 200 feet under me. He saw me at the same moment and turned East, I followed and when he put his nose down I opened fire [from] dead behind from 125 yards range. The observer ceased firing and the machine skidded to the left, in the second burst the left top and then bottom plane, and a little lower the right planes and tail, fell off. He fell East of Passchendaele.[14]

Note how he sensibly turned tail when he "saw 10 enemy scouts coming from SE" — skipping back toward friendly air space, then returning at a greater height ten minutes later. There is a ring of truth to this report which is often lacking in his others. He told Margaret that "it was about 4 miles over [the lines] & I am just waiting to hear if Archie [antiaircraft gunners] saw it." Apparently none of them did — there were no witnesses mentioned in his combat report — but, since he was now CO, he did not hesitate to confirm his own success.

We are fortunate to have a simple numerical chart of enemy losses in the air between March and September 1918, prepared by the German official historians of the First World War.[15] The detailed documentation upon which their count was based was destroyed by British bombing during the Second World War, but there is no reason to disbelieve their figures, which were accumulated before the damage was done. Their chart shows that on 27 May, the enemy lost four machines in their *4 Armee* area — which stretched from the North Sea coast to a point two or three miles north of Armentières and lay opposite 85 Squadron's field at Petit Synthe, near Dunkirk — and one in the 6 *Armee* domain, which reached as far south as Vimy.

Aircraft, of course, were not expected to adhere strictly to army boundaries, and fighters in particular would range further afield when in hot pursuit. Still, they were not likely to go further than the neighbouring army's more distant boundary, while two-seaters, used for artillery spotting and tactical reconnaissance, could be expected to stay close to their assigned targets. Unfortunately, the chart does not identify losses by type, but Bishop's victory, if it was genuine, must have been one of those five losses. And if it fell "E of Passchaendale," it was almost certainly one of the four lost in 4 *Armee* area.

However, other RAF pilots claimed at least six victims in the same area on the 27th. Captain P.J. Clayson and Second Lieutenant E.T.S. Kelly of Number 1 Squadron, stationed seventeen miles south of Petit Synthe, shared in the destruction of two two-seaters — one in flames in the Kemmel-Bailleul area during an afternoon patrol — and Clayson claimed an Albatros D-V destroyed over Steenwerck in the evening. Captain C.G. Ross of 29 Squadron, based at St. Omer, about twenty miles south of Petit Synthe, claimed a two-seater in flames southeast of Bailleul. Lieutenant A.T. Thayer of 20 Squadron and his observer/gunner, Airman First Class A. Newlands, destroyed a Pfalz D-III just south of Neuve Eglise. And Captain W.S. Jenkins of 210 Squadron accounted for another Albatros D-V east of Ypres.[16] If we include Bishop's claim, that makes seven, and at least two of them must have been mistaken or false. These claims, and all the later ones cited, take no account of the many opponents allegedly driven down out of control; nor do they include claims submitted by pilots who never achieved "ace" status, since those listed by my authorities (Shores, Franks and Guest) only deal with those made by men who eventually became aces.

(It may be argued that the German figures are not reliable, even though they appear in the official history. It is, of course, no longer possible to check their reckoning, but it seems very unlikely that the Germans' official historians were fudging the numbers. By and large, everyone's losses were comparatively low during Bishop's brief second tour, since nothing much was happening at the northern end of the front. The great German spring offensives had failed and the Allied counterattacks had not yet begun; thus there was no reason for the air arms to exert themselves unduly and they remained relatively quiescent. But during those German historians had admitted much greater losses — twenty-four by 7 *Armee* on 21 March 1918 and twenty-five on 2 June, for example. And when 2 *Armee* had to stem the RAF onslaught at Amiens on 8 and 9 August, it would record the loss of eighty-eight machines in two days! These are not the figures of men endeavouring to deceive.)

The next day, 28 May, Bishop reported picking off the last two of a formation of nine Albatros D-Vs southwest of Cortemarck, both of which "burst into flames," putting his score up to fifty. Then he flew away, easily escaping the remaining seven.[17] What a difference between ten enemy scouts and nine! Only the day before, he had wisely fled from a formation of ten. However, 4 *Armee* lost eight aircraft that day, and the numbers claimed and lost offer no factual basis on which to question his story. He now had fifty victories, which left him seven behind McCudden, who, after being awarded a VC to add to his DSO and Bar, MC and Bar (which put him one "gong" ahead of Bishop) had been withdrawn from the front early in March and was currently instructing at Ayr.

Aside from the social aspects of life — and it seems to have been a *very* social squadron, with eggnog being mixed by the pailful,[18] driven primarily by the private means of Horn, Springs and Callahan — Bishop was spending very little time with his officers. On 30 May, he told Margaret that "this morning I led a patrol just over the lines, to give some of the new people a bit of experience. No Huns were about." But they were there in the late afternoon while he was flying alone once again:

> Whilst watching a patrol of enemy scouts I was attacked by two-seaters from in front and above. I dived and zoomed up at right hand one, firing a short burst from 60 yards. He passed over me and fell out of control in a left-handed spiral, fell to bits [at] about 10,000 feet and burst into flames on crashing between Roulers and Rumbeke. I then recovered position under second EA's tail, who immediately dived. I fired several short bursts on [illegible] him. At 145 to 150 mph his left plane folded up, followed by his right. I then chased third EA who was 1,000 feet higher from East of Ypres to St. Omer but was unable to climb up to him as he increased his height.[19]

This is a curious story, questionable in the light of common sense and the usual German tactics. Two-seaters did not normally initiate attacks on scouts, nor could one be expected to successfully outclimb a fighter. The only two-seater in the German inventory that might have escaped by thwarting Bishop in terms of height, given a head start so to speak, was the LVG C-VI, which had an operational ceiling of 21,320 feet — but the SE 5a could theoretically reach 22,000 feet. It seems likely that most, if not all, of Bishop's imaginary claims were based upon some real encounter — and they usually made sense on the surface — but in this case the alleged engagement makes no sense at all.

Later that evening, on another solitary sortie, he attacked a pair of Albatroses. Taking the top one first, "I opened fire while in a turn, firing 20 rounds. E.A. fell and crashed 1/2 mile N.W. of Armentières." One wonders what the range was. To bring down an opponent with only twenty rounds while in the midst of a turn speaks extraordinarily highly of his deflection shooting — if the story is true. He fired thirty rounds at the second one from 200 yards and "E.A. went into a spin which I think was controlled." He made no claim for this second machine.[20]

During the day, 4 *Armee* had lost three machines, while 6 *Armee* did not lose any. Were all three Bishop's victims? Perhaps, but Mannock's protégé, Ira Jones of 74 Squadron at La Lovie — eighteen miles southeast of Petit Synthe — was also credited with two two-seaters this day: an LVG and a Halberstadt, destroyed east of Bailleul and southeast of the Bois du Biez, respectively. A little further afield, Captain A.C. Atkey and Lieutenant C.G. Gass of 22 Squadron in their Bristol Fighter destroyed a Pfalz D-III, and Captain F.J. Davies of 29 Squadron claimed an Albatros D-V. Both of these over Armentières.

That evening, in his usual letter to Margaret, Bishop explained: "I'm too worried to write much tonight. Lobo went out by himself tonight at 7 o'clock & has not returned. It is now 10 minutes to 10 and he only has a little over 2 hrs petrol."[21] "Lobo" was one of his flight commanders, Edwin Benbow, with eight victories to his credit from an earlier tour. Bishop had often shown a degree of callousness over his less fortunate comrades in his earlier letters, when he bothered to mention them at all — it may well have been part of his psychological protection against the cold winds of mortality — but Benbow seems to have constituted an exception. Was he genuinely upset, or was his concern more a matter of appearances for Margaret's sake? Since coming to

England, she had met all his pilots and he may have recognized a need to appear concerned over the loss of someone she knew. The next day:

> We learned today that poor old Lobo, bless him, was killed last night. He fell just inside our lines. His funeral is tomorrow. I would like to go, but I don't think I shall, and I'm not allowing any of the flying officers to go. It is too upsetting.... Three Huns surprised him & fought him for sometime, finally shooting his wings off & he fell, of course killed instantly. He was not quite up-to-date, I'm afraid, too long out of it, poor Lobo he was a white man through & through, and the squadron loved him as I did.[22]

"Archie called up and said they saw him [Benbow] coming out of Hunland with five Huns on his tail," noted Grider in his diary. "Just as he got to the lines two of them fired a burst and his plane dived into the ground on our side of the lines."[23] Since the SE was faster than any Pfalz in level flight, and Benbow was shot down at a low level, it would seem that the enemy machines had used an initial height advantage to build up speed and catch him. He had been "too long out of it" for only a little over a year, having finished a tour with 40 Squadron in March 1917. Bishop had also been away from combat for nearly ten months, but he was still quite cautious in his re-approach to the enemy. "Tonight I took Horn & Springs up to look at the lines, just to have a look," he had written on the 26th. "I saw 4 Huns and then one alone. Longed to dash down on him, but I want to study their tactics, so I kept this side [of the lines]."[24]

On 31 May, when *4 Armee* lost six machines, Grider recorded (in a diary entry dated 3 June) that "they are changing the score now as the major has just come down and has shot down two more Huns — a scout and a two-seater ... and now has more than McCudden. Archie saw one of them go down and another one broke up in the air."[25]

Bishop's version was somewhat different. In his first combat report of the day, he recorded that he had "attacked one of 3 Pfalz scouts sitting about 2,000 feet above a formation of about 14 E.A. I fired 20 rounds at 20 yards range from behind. E.A. immediately fell completely out of control. I was unable to watch it owing to the presence of the remainder of the E.A. formation." As was now almost always the case, he was flying alone, and apparently no one else saw his victim fall, but RAF Communiqué Number 31.5 decided — perhaps not unreasonably, given the alleged range — that his target had been destroyed. He next "attacked a two-seater E.A.... I fired a long burst from rear at 100 yards range, E.A. turned to left, then dived East and landed in a field."[26] Oddly, this time no claim was made, nor was credit given — perhaps the enemy machine was classified as "driven down *under* control."

A second report of an evening flight saw him claim an unidentified aircraft that "fell to bits," adding that "this EA must have been seen by A[nti-] A[ircraft] Batteries of the 2nd Army as visibility was very good."[27]

McCudden had now replaced Ball as Bishop's rival. His score was now fifty-seven, but as Bishop informed Margaret:

> Today I got two more, one this afternoon. I sent a Pfalz scout down out of control, opened fire at him from 20 yds range and riddled the damn pilot. Later I attacked a two seater & killed his observer,

I think. Anyway, he landed in a field. This evening
I went out and while watching this side of the
lines, along came 2 Pfalz to attack balloons. They
turned and fled but I caught one 2 miles over, and
he was so terrified he never even attempted a turn.
I shot him to pieces from 50 yds.... My total is
now 55.[28]

The next day, 1 June, while flying alone as usual, by chance he
met up with Horn, Springs and McGregor, and together they inter-
cepted a formation of six black-painted Pfalz fighters. "Into them
we waded & I got one crashed. McGregor got two out of control &
Springs got one."[29] Grider, who wrote a more detailed account in
his diary, must have talked with one or more of the three.

Just after they crossed the lines, Bish joined them
and led them down on the same six Huns at the
same place where Springs found them before, and
at the same hour. They must have been the same
ones that got Benbow. Methodical, these Huns
are. They were in two layers of three each. Bish
and Mac took the lower ones and Springs and
Nigger [Horn] took the top ones. Bish and Mac
each got one and Springs got one down out of
control but no one saw it crash so he doesn't
score.... They were Pfalz scouts and are easy meat
for SEs.[30]

That day, 4 Armee recorded losing five machines, 6 Armee another five — apparently providing enough victims to satisfy all claims —
and Bishop noted on his own combat report that "Lieut. Springs con-

firms the E.A. I shot down" over La Gorgue.[31] (Apparently Grider was wrong about Springs not scoring; his combat report, countersigned by Bishop, recorded "1 out of control.")

Bishop claimed two Albatros scouts in a span of ten minutes on 4 June. He was out alone again, near the coast at 14,000 feet, when, "seeing a formation of 8 E.A. out to sea, I flew towards them from the East & diving, attacked a straggler, after 10 rounds from each gun he burst into flames and fell burning brightly. I zoomed away and escaped." Following them inland, "I attacked another straggler of the same formation" at a height of 15,000 feet. This one, after absorbing "30 rounds from each gun at 75 yards range … fell completely out of control and passed through clouds 8,000 feet below still out of control."

The second victim, at least, was a very doubtful case. Bishop was an excellent shot and should have caused serious, if not fatal, damage to his foe had the combat developed as he claimed, but with 7,000 feet still to fall when last seen, his victim may or may not have been genuinely out of control. Other evidence suggests that he was not. *4 Armee*, which was closest to the coast, lost only one aircraft on 4 June, and Captain F.R. Smith and Lieutenant W.Q. Adams of 2 Squadron (Australian Flying Corps) shared in the outright destruction of a Fokker D-VII over Capinghem that evening.

On the 5th, the squadron, with Bishop leading, "escorted a bomb raid and went all the way to Holland" without meeting the enemy.[32] The next three days were also uneventful as far as Bishop was concerned. On 9 June, however, the squadron was put on standby, ready for a move south to a more intense environment. The executive order came at noon, and the whole squadron was packed and moving in "less than 3 hrs."

They travelled the short distance to St. Omer and flew the first patrol from their new base that evening. Bishop, however, seems to have stayed on the ground, then and over the next two days, entertaining his wing commander on the 11th and "putting all my gadgets, etc.," on a new machine on the 13th. What he was doing on the 12th went unrecorded. Perhaps, as CO, he was swamped with administration concerned with the move.

The weather was poor on 14 June and there was no flying, but on the 15th he was out during the evening, finding four adversaries, two Pfalz and two Albatroses, "sitting above a large formation of E.A." at 17,500 feet. "In course of combat I fired at 3 of the 4, finally shooting one Pfalz down in flames from 50 yards range and behind," east of Estaires.[33] However, only one German aircraft, belonging to *4 Armee*, was lost during the day (neither *6 Armee* nor *17 Armee* to the south of it lost any), while at least two other RAF aces laid claim to victories at this northern end of the battlefront: Captain T.C. Luke of 209 Squadron reported destroying an Albatros D-III west of Houlthem, while Lieutenant F.C. Howe, 74 Squadron, claimed a Pfalz D-III south of Zillebeke Lake. Both claims were geographically more likely than Bishop's, but even so they could not both be true.

The next day, Bishop was told that he was being recalled to England at the request of the Canadian government. "I have never been so furious in my life. McCudden is to take my place & the squadron is on the verge of mutiny."[34] He was wrong about McCudden. Grider's diary records that:

> The General [Salmond in this case] came over and had tea with us and asked us who we wanted for CO. He wanted to send us McCudden but we don't want him. He gets Huns himself but he doesn't give anybody else a chance at them…. We asked for Micky Mannock who is a flight com-

mander in 74 [Squadron]. He's got around sixty
Huns and was at London Colney when we were,
in January. He wanted to take the three of us out
with him in February but we weren't thru at
Turnberry. They say that he's the best patrol leader
at the front — plans his squadron shows a day in
advance and rehearses them on the ground. He
plans every manoeuvre like a chess player and has
every man at a certain place at a certain time to do
a certain thing, and raises merry hell if anyone
falls down on his job.[35]

*"He gets Huns himself but doesn't give anybody else a chance
at them."* Given his current commander's plain lack of interest
in advancing the careers of any of his pilots, that is a bizarre
comment. How could anyone in 85 Squadron think that Bishop
was not the supreme exponent of that attitude? At least the
squadron got its wish in the person of Mannock, who had a ster-
ling reputation for nursing his pilots along and sharing his kills
with them.

Posted back to England, Bishop had probably brought his fate
upon himself. The agitation for a Canadian air force had never
entirely ceased, and it had developed new momentum when Sir
A.E. Kemp had replaced Sir George Perley as overseas minister in
October 1917. Sir Richard Turner was as keen as ever and Sir
Arthur Currie, the commander of the Canadian Corps in France,
had joined the crusade in November 1917, writing to Turner that
"because you and I have never discussed the formation of a
Canadian Flying Corps, I do not know what your views are con-

cerning such a step, but in my opinion such a thing is desirable."[36] Then, as Canada's premier fighter pilot and most famous airman, Bishop had personally weighed in while he was still in England in an April letter to Major General E.W.B. Morrison, the pre-war journalist and militia officer who now commanded the Canadian Corps artillery in France and who was also pushing for a Canadian air service. Claiming to speak for all his compatriots in the RAF, he wrote:

> Under the present circumstances, Canadians in the RAF, although doing remarkably well, are certainly not doing as well as if they were in a Canadian Corps for the reasons that (1) They are in a great many cases working under senior Officers who do not understand them. (2) They are also working with Officers who do not understand them nor often appreciate their different point of view. (3) They have not the personal touch with their country which branches of the Canadian Corps have and consequently are not inspired by direct connection with the country they are fighting for and the people at home.[37]

Perhaps a third of the airmen on the Western Front were Canadian, and in London the RAF was fighting a desperate delaying action, recognizing that drafting them into a new establishment would inevitably cause confusion and disruption on a vast scale just as the air war seemed to be reaching a climax. Canadians, too, understood this, and a compromise was reached in a meeting at the Air Ministry on 28 May 1918: the British would not object to a nominal Canadian air force of two squadrons for the present, while a running record would be established of those Canadians remaining in the RAF and they would be permitted to wear "Canada" badges on their uniforms.

A decision to raise the two squadrons, one fighter and one bomber, was made on 5 June, and eleven days later Bishop was ordered back to England to take prime responsibility for forming a Canadian wing and to become the overseas minister's senior adviser on questions relating to the organization and the training of the new Canadian Air Force. To that end he would be promoted to temporary lieutenant-colonel and attached to Overseas Military Forces headquarters as head of a CAF section.[38]

Bishop had three days left in which to maximize his score. The evening of the 16th, flying alone yet again, he claimed a two-seater "burst into flames" east of Armentières and, eight minutes later, an Albatros "crashed on western edge of Armentières."[39] At St. Omer the squadron was positioned roughly opposite the boundary between 4 *Armee* and 6 *Armee*, the two northernmost German armies, each of which lost two aircraft that day. Captain E.T. Hayne of 203 Squadron shared a Pfalz D-III with seven of his colleagues over Estaires, an indisputable victory with *eight* eyewitnesses, and Mannock claimed another, three miles south of Zillebeke Lake, while Lieutenant William Sidebottom was credited with destroying a two-seater, also over Estaires. Finally, Lieutenant D.E. Smith and his observer/gunner, in a Bristol Fighter, were credited with another Pfalz south of Comines. Leaving that certain 203 Squadron kill out of the equation, there were five claims, one of them with two witnesses, but only three losses. Somebody was overclaiming, as usual. Could it have been Major Bishop?

The next morning, he claimed three in the course of another solitary flight before the weather closed in, all three far over the lines: a two-seater that "burst into flames" in the vicinity of Staden and Hooglede' a solitary Albatros "crashed just South of Sailly-sur-le-Lys"; and a second two-seater crashed "between Laventie and main road," this last being his sixty-fifth victory.[40] None were witnessed. Seven enemy aircraft were lost in the precincts of the two northern armies, where Bishop's claims lay, and without going into boring detail (those who distrust my figures can study the source book for themselves), at least twelve victories in addition to Bishop's three were claimed and credited in the same area. Fifteen claims and only seven losses.

On the 18th, Bishop claimed two more.

> While looking for one of the Squadron patrols I saw 4 E.A., seen thru a gap in the clouds circling around each other. I dived into the cloud and came out in the gap just above them, secured a position on tail of one. After very short burst he seemed to explode and went down in flames. At same moment one of the other 3 spun away, of the remaining two, one attacked me, the other firing wildly from 300 yards on one side. I fired a long burst in a deflection shot at E.A. fighting me, and he smoked then burst into flames. 4th E.A. then spun away and I fired 20 rounds at him with no result.[41]

Again there were no witnesses, but seven German aircraft were lost this day and I can only identify five other pilots credited with one victory each — one of them being his wife's brother, Lieutenant Henry Burden. Thus, both of these claims *may* have been valid, although, as pointed out earlier, the victories listed in *Above the Trenches* which I have employed to question many of his 1918 claims only relate to those airmen who eventually became aces. A considerable number of British pilots registered one or two successes before being killed, wounded or taken prisoner themselves, and it is quite possible, even likely, that one or both of the remaining two were credited to one or two of them. Nor does that total of seven consider any aircraft that may have fallen victim to antiaircraft fire.

That day also brought "Mac" Grider's death, in circumstances that hardly reflect any credit on his squadron and flight commanders and add a note of pathos to Grider's diary entry of two days earlier about Mannock being so careful of his pilots and planning every move. Bishop's concern, as always, was primarily with himself. On this occasion, Springs and Grider were patrolling together — two virtual novices who had only been at the front for three weeks! Had Bishop been posted a week earlier and Mannock been their commanding officer, they would never have been flying alone so soon after reaching the front.

> Mac and I were up over the lines and we saw a German two-seater about five miles away and about 12,000 feet. We attacked it and succeeded in shooting it down. By that time we were from 15 to 20 miles in Hunland, so we started back at full speed. Mac was just behind and I saw him following me. However, I got lost several times before I got back and that is the last I ever saw of him.[42]

In the summer of 1918, anything less than a full squadron venturing so far over the enemy lines was an invitation to disaster —

and that fact should have been drilled into them over the past three weeks. The two of them should never have allowed themselves to be drawn so deep into German airspace. Finally, since their machines were faster in level flight than anything the enemy had in the air — their likeliest opponent, a Fokker D-VII, was 10 mph slower — they should never have been caught from behind; presumably, Grider's nemesis either dived on him, with the necessary speed coming from an advantage of height, or came in at an angle that negated the SE 5's superior speed.

The next day, 19 June, was Bishop's last day of battle and he ended his First World War exploits with a single, solitary morning sortie in which he claimed *five* victories in the course of half an hour. It was a very cloudy morning in which enemy aircraft were rather unlikely to be abroad. However:

> 1,100 feet. 1 mile E. of Ploegsteert. 9.38 a.m.
>
> After crossing the lines in the clouds I came out over Ploegsteert Wood, saw 3 Pfalz Scouts which I attacked. 2 other Pfalz then approached from the East. I fired short burst into one of original 3. He went down in vertical dive [from 1,100 feet]. 2nd and 3rd E.A. then while circling about me collided and fell together. 1st E.A. crashed and burst into flames 1 mile E. of Ploegsteert. Remaining 2 E.A. turned and flew E. I gave chase and opened fire on one at 200 yards range. E.A. spun into ground. Last E.A. zoomed up into clouds and escaped.
>
> 900 feet. Between Neuve Eglise & Ploegsteert at 10.10 a.m.
>
> I met a two-seater and attacked from behind and underneath. E.A. burst into flames. I then fired on a

small body of troops on the ground scattering them. Climbed into clouds and flew West.[43]

The first thing to be noted here is that it was most unusual, if not unique, for an airman to be credited with aircraft that collided with each other while manoeuvring to attack him. It was not a rare event for either side to suffer such misfortune (the great Boelcke had died in exactly such circumstances), but I know of no previous case in which the object of their manoeuvres was credited with their destruction.*

The second point is that the three northernmost German armies only lost *one* machine between them this day, that one being from 4 *Armee*, (although Captain J.E. Gurdon of 22 Squadron and his observer/gunner, 2nd Lieutenant J.J. Scaramanga, were also credited with destroying *two* Fokker D-VIIs over Armentières, near the boundary of 4 and 6 *Armees*). Moreover, by the standards generally applied, two of Bishop's five, which he described as having "collided and fell together," should not have been credited to him and the three others could, at best, have only been one. Even that seems unlikely.

---

* Although another exception would subsequently be made in the case of fellow Canadian Raymond Collishaw, who was credited with two which "collided, and spun into cloud locked together" on 22 July 1918.

Date	Sortie Number	Claim in Combat Report or Logbook	Location	Patrol or Alone	Official Dispostition	Victory No.	Witness
26/5/18	185	"To look at the lines"	?	Alone			
27/5/18	186	"To look at the lines"	?	Alone			
"	187	"Wings and tail fell off"	E of Passchendaele	Alone	Destroyed*	48	No
28/5/18	188	Enemy seen — not engaged	Passchendaele	Alone			
"	189	"OOC, then in flames"	SW of Cortemarck	Alone	Destroyed	49	No
"	190	E.A "in flames"	SW of Cortemarck	Alone	Destroyed	50	No
30/5/18	191	"No enemy seen"	Line Patrol	Patrol			
"	192	"Fell and crashed"	Armentières	Alone	Destroyed*	51	No
"	"	"OOC, then in flames"	Roulers	Alone	Destroyed*	52	No
"	193	"Wings fell off"	Rumbeke	Alone	Destroyed*	53	No
31/5/18	194	No enemy reported	?	Alone			
"	195	"Completely out of control"	Quesnoy	Alone	Destroyed	54	No
"	196	"E.A. fell to bits"	N of Estaires	Alone	Destroyed	55	No
1/6/18	197	Enemy seen — not engaged	Near Ypres	Alone			
"	198	"E/A. spun and crashed"	La Gorgue	Patrol	Destroyed	56	No
2/6/18	199	"E/A broke into pieces"	S of Armentières	Patrol	Destroyed	57	Yes
4/6/18	200	"He burst into flames"	Nieuport–Ostend	Alone	Destroyed*	58	No
"	"	"Completely out of control"	Leffinge	Alone	Destroyed*	59	No
"	201	No enemy reported	Line Patrol	Patrol			
5/6/18	202	No enemy reported	?	Alone			
6/6/18	203	No enemy reported	Bomber escort	Patrol			

Date	No.	Claim	Location		Result		
"	204	No enemy reported	?	Alone			
15/6/18	202	Enemy seen — not engaged	E of Estaires	Alone			
"	203	"Down in flames"	E of Estaires	Alone	Destroyed*	60	No
16/6/18	204	"Burst into flames"	E of Armentières	Alone	Destroyed*	61	No
"	"	"Crashed"	Over Armentières	Alone	Destroyed*	62	No
17/6/18	205	"Burst into flames"	Staden/Hooglede	Alone	Destroyed*	63	No
"	"	"Fell and crashed"	Sailly-sur-le-Lys	Alone	Destroyed*	64	No
"	"	"Fell … then crashed"	Near Laventie	Alone	Destroyed*	65	No
18/6/18	206	"Went down in flames"	NE of Ypres	Alone	Destroyed*	66	No
"	"	"Burst into flames"	NE of Ypres	Alone	Destroyed*	67	No
19/6/18	207	"In vertical dive"	Ploegsteert	Alone	Destroyed†	68	No
"	"	E.A. "collided and fell together"	Ploegsteert	Alone	Destroyed†	69	No
"	"	E.A. "collided and fell together"	Ploegsteert	Alone	Destroyed†	70	No
"	"	"EA spun into ground"	Ploegsteert	Alone	Destroyed†	71	No
"	"	"Burst into flames"	Neuve Eglise	Alone	Destroyed†	72	No

*Doubtful or false on the basis of known German losses and other RAF claims.
†Four of five certainly false on the basis of known German losses.

While leading patrols of 85 Squadron, Bishop flew only five sorties, and on three of them no enemies were seen. Twice, hostile aircraft were observed in the distance but not engaged. He had two fights and claimed two victories, one of which was witnessed by Elliot Springs. Flying alone, however, he managed 21 sorties, on five of which no adversaries were observed, while on three they were seen but not encountered. He reported being engaged in 23 fights (if we include the two machines that collided as two fights) and claimed 23 victories. Whether flying in company or alone, he appears to have a phenomenal ratio of fights to victories during the last twenty-four days of his operational career. The end result of all this was a total of 72 victories amassed in a relatively brief operational career, making him what he had always desired to be — the British Empire's top-scoring ace. His spectacular success while with 85 Squadron would bring him yet another decoration, one of the new Distinguished Flying Crosses, introduced to meet the demands of the now-independent Royal Air Force, but there would be no Bar to his VC.

Epilogue

In the eighty-four years since his fighting days ended, Billy Bishop has attained mythic status in Canadian eyes. "Most countries choose individuals with larger-than-life qualities to mythologize," according to writer and critic Charlotte Gray.

> Extraordinary imagination, against-the-odds bravery, brilliant creativity. There are colourful characters in our collective past who embody such qualities — think of Sir Sandford Fleming, inventor of Standard Time; Dr. Frederick Banting, co-discoverer of insulin; the fighter pilot Billy Bishop. Why aren't they on our money, instead of stuffy old Mackenzie King?... The political and military heroes of other countries are celebrated for their fierce individualism and driving determination. But these are not Canadian qualities: Canada is not a militaristic nation.[1]

A week later, however, Ms. Gray, without going into any detail, also managed to include Bishop in a list of bogus characters that embraced Laura Secord, a "heroine" of the War of 1812 whose probably fictitious exploit is now commemorated by a chocolate candy franchise; Archie Belaney, the Englishman who masqueraded as Grey Owl, a full-blooded Indian conservationist; and Lili St. Cyr, the "French-Canadian" striptease *artiste* who was actually from Minneapolis and whose real name was Marie Van Schaak![2]

An Internet poll of researchers and interested parties taken early in 1999 also reflected mixed feelings about the Bishop legend. Three hundred and eighty-five respondents thought that he deserved his VC, 172 thought not, and 40 were undecided.[3]

Bishop *was* a hero — anyone who flew as much as he did in 1917, when the odds were so heavily stacked against him, was a hero almost by definition. (Although he was not nearly such a hero as he claimed to be.) He encapsulated all of the heroic qualities listed by Gray — extraordinary imagination, brilliant creativity (did Ms. Gray realize what she was saying?), against-the-odds bravery, fierce individualism and driving determination. Ranked ninth in that all-time list of Canadian heroes mentioned in the introduction, Bishop was, and still is, certainly better known than the other two individuals that she initially singled out, Fleming and Banting. Generations of Canadian boys, inspired by romantic ideas of war, have grown up dreaming of emulating him. His hometown of Owen Sound, Ontario, has a museum devoted to his exploits and the Canadian Forces Air Command named its headquarters building in Winnipeg in his honour.

Too little attention is paid to the First World War in Canadian school history books, but whenever the topic is raised Bishop is likely to be front and centre among Canadian personalities associated with it. Today, it may well be — it is even likely — that more Canadians are familiar with his name than that of Sir Arthur

Currie, who commanded the Canadian Corps and, judging by results, was the best general Canada has yet produced.

Currie had a substantial blot on his record, too, but it was just one blot.[4] Bishop's career shows a pattern of lying and deceitfulness, starting with his cheating at the Royal Military College, and carrying on through such relatively minor deceptions as telling Princess Marie Louise that his sister had been named after her, revising his medical history to make it a little less mundane, and awarding himself a campaign medal to which he was not entitled, to more significant porkies which include his spurious account of battling the Red Baron, his claim to have shot down three German aircraft after strafing a German airfield, and the destruction of twenty-five adversaries in twenty-three days in the course of his second tour at the front.

Bishop was a born mythomaniac, but he was also an extraordinarily lucky man. Only one thing could have served his cause better than his crossing paths with Lady St. Helier, and that was his good fortune to have been posted to Jack Scott's squadron. St. Helier had immeasurable social and political influence, Scott had social and military leverage out of all proportion to his service rank, and both, for their own very different reasons, were more than happy to advance his career. No less auspicious was Bishop's arrival on the Western Front (as a fighter pilot) at a time when the Royal Flying Corps was desperate to create aces who could serve as role models and help restore the Corps' sagging morale.

It is surely worth reiterating how brave Bishop was, particularly in those early months when he was learning his trade. Only a brave man would fly at all in 1917–18; only a very brave man would fly alone; and only an unbelievably brave man would consistently venture beyond the enemy's front line at such a disadvantage. Bishop not only did so, but apparently sometimes flew deep into German airspace (though, because he was alone, we can never be sure how far he penetrated) relying on keen eyes, assiduous concentration and situational awareness to keep him alive.

He was also just plain lucky in the field, particularly during his early days with 60 Squadron. His first undoubted victory came in the course of a long, high-speed dive that should have ripped the wings off his lightly-built machine and carried him to his death, but did not.

In the course of 208 operational sorties and some 110 fights over a period of ninety-four days at the front, he was credited with seventy-two enemy aircraft destroyed or driven down out of control — very nearly one in every three sorties and one in every 1.5 fights. The victory that he originally claimed to have shared with Willie Fry on 4 May 1917, but subsequently took full credit for, is included in that total, although in the light of Fry's later evidence (see Chapter 4), only a desire not to do him an injustice leads me to take his word about that ambiguous and baffling case and include it as a witnessed victory. Doing so means that five of his victories were corroborated by eyewitnesses according to the written record; and all five occurred while he was flying in company, although the first two, observed from the ground, could equally well have been witnessed while flying alone.

That first, indisputable, victory came on 27 March 1917 and, during the seven weeks of operational flying between then and 31 May (he was on leave for two weeks), he claimed twenty-one more — ten while flying in company and eleven while flying alone. His second victory was also witnessed, but three of those claimed while flying in company and five while flying alone were extremely doubtful, in that no witnesses were recorded and Scott's dispositions clearly exaggerated Bishop's descriptions of the combats. In June, he claimed only one while in company, but eight — including the three on 2 June — while flying alone. Then, in the final seven weeks of his sojourn with 60 Squadron, he claimed six while in company and ten while flying alone.

Altogether, eleven of the forty-three victories (excluding the four witnessed ones) claimed while he was at Izel-le-Hameau may have been genuine. But, as we have just noted, the words Bishop used in the relevant combat reports suggest they were much more often a consequence of Scott's enthusiasm than his own prowess. We might reasonably conclude, on a balance of probabilities, that certainly no more than a third of them — say, four of the eleven — were valid, and it is very possible that they were all false. Of the remaining thirty-two claims, more clearly stated, eighteen were allegedly destroyed and eleven driven down out of control, with no witnesses advanced for any of them. Because of the paucity of German records, it is simply not possible to argue with any certainty whether they were genuine or not, but it should be noted how the language of Bishop's reports changed to reflect the certainties that Scott had used in confirming his earlier reports. He was a quick study.

If reliable German records for the summer of 1917 did exist, they would certainly show a somewhat more balanced ratio of officially credited RFC/RNAS victories to enemy losses than the 1918 figures, just as those for 1916 would have been still closer to the true facts. Each year the concentrations of planes in the air increased, speeds rose, manoeuvrability improved, and pilots found themselves with less time to evaluate what was happening around them, making it progressively harder for them to make accurate assessments of their efforts, no matter how honest their intentions. Moreover, as the war developed and propaganda began to play a greater part — both in the services and on the home front — wing, brigade and higher headquarters became less and less rigorous in their standards of acceptance.

Thus, with the benefit of hindsight, we know that a degree of excessive claiming was becoming common by the spring and summer of 1917, and all we know of Bishop makes it unlikely that he would have been one of the more conservative claimants. Set against this background, perhaps a benevolent assumption would be that eight or nine were actually destroyed and no more than two or three of those allegedly driven down were truly out of control. Let us say, then, that eleven of the twenty-nine were genuine. That yields a total of nineteen victories while with 60 Squadron.

When Bishop returned to the fray in 1918, he brazenly claimed twenty-five victories, all but one (corroborated by Springs, an admiring and perhaps not impeccable witness) while flying alone, four of which we know from the established figures of German losses must have been wrong, and most of which were highly questionable despite the fact that they were all claimed as destroyed and none as driven down.

Four of the five claims from his last sortie on 19 June 1918, when the three German armies on the northern end of the Western Front lost only one aircraft among them, were clearly false. Even granting him the fifth of the five means denying it to the Bristol Fighter pilot and gunner who claimed to have destroyed two, with at least one of their claims necessarily being false. But although there were two of them and only one of him, Bishop's claim is perhaps as good as theirs.

Of the remaining twenty-one claims made while he was commanding 85 Squadron, there is no good reason — other than his falsification in other cases — to deny six (even though he was flying alone), but fifteen are highly questionable in the light of known German losses and claims made by other RAF pilots. German losses on the British front in May and June 1918 were about half the number of victories credited to British airmen,[5] so pilots were claiming — on average — twice the number that they were truly entitled to. Let us, then, on the aforementioned balance of probabilities, grant Bishop half of the initial six and a third of the remaining fifteen. Altogether, eight out of twenty-five, and, adding the nineteen from 60 Squadron, a total of twenty-seven!

The official figure was seventy-two; McCaffery, in *Billy Bishop, Canadian Hero*, discounts "about two dozen" of Bishop's claims, which would leave him with about forty-eight,[6] and Graves, in *World War II Investigator*, proposed a total score of twenty-three.[7] If my assessments are correct (and the reader must judge that for himself), Bishop's final tally was far less than McCaffery's assumption, a little more than Graves suggests, and slightly more than a third of the victories credited to him.

That puts a half-dozen or more aces — whose claims were better attested to — ahead of him in the scoring race. Certainly, both McCudden and Mannock must have exceeded his total, with the former claiming fifty-five (of which at least nineteen fell within the British lines, while many, if not most, others were witnessed[8]) and the latter apparently accounting for sixty-one, even though his posthumous VC citation only mentioned fifty. "Exhaustive research has provided details of nearly all the fifty victories credited to Mannock ... [whose] claims have proved verifiable to an above average extent from German records."[9] Among Canadians, Raymond Collishaw, with sixty officially to his credit (two that collided certainly being unwarranted), and W.G. Barker with fifty, both had more witnessed victories than Bishop.

Encouraged and abetted by his superiors, his reputation enthusiastically enhanced by Lady St. Helier and her socially and politically important allies, and his claims unquestioned by doubting comrades reluctant to challenge him, whatever their reasons, a man of Bishop's unquestioned courage and immense determination could hardly fail to distinguish himself. But I claim that Billy Bishop was a distinguished fraud — *a brave flyer but a bold liar* — and the balance of probabilities seems sufficient to make my case.

Second World War veteran Paul Fussell has argued, in a literary study of *his* war, that:

> The damage the war visited upon bodies and build-
> ings, planes and tanks and ships, is obvious. Less
> obvious is the damage it did to intellect, discrimina-
> tion, honesty, individuality, complexity, ambiguity,
> and irony, not to mention privacy and wit. For the
> past fifty years the Allied war has been sanitized and
> romanticized almost beyond recognition by the sen-
> timental, the loony patriotic, the ignorant, and the
> bloodthirsty. I have tried to balance the scales.[10]

I, likewise, have tried to balance the scales, by undoing a little of the damage done to intellect, discrimination and honesty in the First World War. And the same sentimental, loony patriotic, igno-rant or bloodthirsty critics will, no doubt, resent and loudly con-demn both my evidence and conclusions. So be it.

Appendix

Bishop's Citations for British Decorations

Military Cross

For conspicuous gallantry and devotion to duty. He attacked a hostile balloon on the ground, dispersed the crew and destroyed the balloon, and also drove down a hostile machine which attacked him. He has on several other occasions brought down hostile machines.

London Gazette: 30095, 26 May 1917

Distinguished Service Order

For conspicuous gallantry and devotion to duty. While in a single-seater he attacked three hostile machines, two of which he brought down, although in the meantime he was himself attacked by four other hostile machines. His courage and determination have set a fine example to others.

London Gazette: 30135, 18 June 1917

Victoria Cross

For most conspicuous bravery, determination and skill. Captain Bishop, who had been sent out to work independently, flew first of all to an enemy aerodrome, finding no machine about, he flew on to another aerodrome about three miles south-east, which was at least twelve miles the other side of the line. Seven machines, some with their engines running, were on the ground. He attacked these from about fifty feet, and a mechanic who was starting one of the engines was seen to fall. One of the machines got off the ground, but at a height of sixty feet Capt. Bishop fired fifteen rounds into it at very close range and it crashed to the ground.

A second machine got off the ground, into which he fired thirty rounds at 150 yards range, and it fell into a tree. Two more machines then rose from the aerodrome. One of these he engaged at the height of 1,000 feet, emptying the rest of his drum of ammunition. This machine crashed 300 yards from the aerodrome; after which Capt. Bishop emptied a whole drum into the fourth machine and then flew back to his station.

Four hostile scouts were about 1,000 feet above him for about a mile of his return journey, but they would not attack.

His machine was very badly shot about by machine-gun fire from the ground.

London Gazette: 30228, 11 August 1917

Bar to DSO

For conspicuous gallantry and devotion to duty when engaging hostile aircraft. His consistent dash and great fearlessness have set a magnificent example to the pilots of his squadron. Has destroyed no less than 45 hostile machines within the past five months, frequently attacking enemy formations sin-glehanded and on all occasions displaying a fighting spirit and determination to get to close quarters with his opponents which have earned the admiration of all in contact with him.

London Gazette: 30466, 9 January 1918

Distinguished Flying Cross

A most successful and fearless fighter in the air, his acts of outstanding bravery have already been recognized in the awards of the V.C., D.S.O., Bar to the D.S.O., and the M.C.

For the award of the D.F.C. now conferred upon him he has rendered signally valuable services in personally destroy-ing twenty-five enemy machines in twelve days — five of which he destroyed on the last day of his service at the front.

The total number of machines destroyed by this distin-guished officer is seventy-two, and his value as a moral fac-tor to the Royal Air Force cannot be overestimated.

London Gazette: 30827, 3 August 1918

ENDNOTES

Introduction

1. M.J. Crook, *The Evolution of the Victoria Cross: A Study in Administrative History* (Tunbridge Wells, Kent: Midas Books, 1975), p. 21.

2. Ibid., p. 173.

3. Ibid., pp. 270–71. See also Richard Garrett, *The Final Betrayal* (Shedfield, Southampton: Buchan & Enright, 1989), p. 205.

4. *National Post*, 30 June 1999, p. A8.

5. Denis Winter, *The First of the Few: Fighter Pilots of the First World War* (Athens, Georgia: University of Georgia Press, 1983), p. 37.

6. John English, *Shadow of Heaven: The Life of Lester Pearson, Vol. I: 1897–1948* (Toronto: Lester & Orpen Dennys, 1989), pp. 43–47.

7. Directorate of History and Heritage, National Defence Headquarters, Ottawa [hereafter DHH], 2001/9, W.A. Bishop Collection, Bishop to Margaret Burden, [illegible] Sept. 1917. With two specified exceptions, copies of all of Bishop's letters subsequently cited are to be found in this collection.

8. DHH, 2001/9, Bishop Collection, Arthur Bishop to Ralph Manning, 8 Jan 1961.

9. S.F. Wise, *Canadian Airmen and the First World War* [Canadian Official History] (Toronto: University of Toronto Press, 1980), p. xv.

10. *New York Times*, 17 May 1980, p. 14.

11. H.C. Chadderton, *Hanging a Legend: The National Film Board's Shameful Attempt to Discredit Billy Bishop, VC* (Ottawa: War Amputations of Canada, n.d.), p. x.

12. Wise, *Canadian Airmen*, p. 574.

13. Norman L.R. Franks, Russell Guest and Frank W. Bailey, *Bloody April — Black September* (London: Grub Street, 1995), p. 4.

14. Wise, *Canadian Airmen*, p. 574.

15. *The Times*, 1 June and 1 July 1918.

16. Christopher Shores, Norman Franks and Russell Guest, *Above the Trenches: A Complete Record of the Fighter Aces and Units of the British Empire Air Forces, 1915–1920* (London: Grub Street 1990), pp. 249–50.

17. Dan McCaffery, *Billy Bishop: Canadian Hero* (Toronto: Lorimer, 1988), p. 209.

18. Ibid., p. 209.

19. Ibid., p. 208.

20. Timothy Graves, "World War I's Flying Aces," in *World War II Investigator*, Vol. 1, No. 8 (November 1988), pp. 7–14.

21. Philip Markham, "The Early Morning Hours of 2 June 1917," in *Over the Front*, Vol.10, No.3 (Fall 1995), p. 251.

22. Crook, *Evolution of the Victoria Cross*, p. 96.

23. H.A. Jones, *The War in the Air*, Vol. III [British Official History] (Oxford: Clarendon Press, 1936), p. 336n.

24. Wise, *Canadian Airmen*, pp. 597–98.

Chapter 1: "The Greatest Game in the World"

1. Arthur Bishop, *The Courage of the Early Morning* (Toronto: McClelland & Stewart, 1965), p. 12.
2. *The Stone Frigate 1914*, RMC Archives, Kingston, Ontario.
3. W.A. Bishop, *Winged Warfare* (Toronto: McClelland, Goodchild & Stewart, 1918), p. 18.
4. RMC Standing Orders, amended to December 1911, para. 120, in RMC Archives.
5. Leonard diary, 28 March 1914, *passim*, 04075-IL in 1st Hussars Museum, London, Ontario.
6. Letters to Margaret Burden, 7, 9 and 14 July 1915.
7. G.W.L. Nicholson, *Canadian Expeditionary Force 1914–1919*, (Ottawa, 1962), p. 113.
8. To Margaret Burden, 25 July 1915.
9. National Archives of Canada [NAC], RG 150, Accession 1992-93/166, file 48.
10. To Margaret Burden, 6 Aug 1915.
11. Ibid., 7 Aug 1915.
12. W.D. Mathieson, *Billy Bishop, VC* (Markham, Ontario: Fitzhenry & Whiteside, 1989), p. 14.
13. Ibid., p. 15.
14. To Margaret Burden, 8, 11 and 17 Nov 1915.
15. Ibid., 14 and 27 Nov 1915.
16. Leonard diary, *loc.cit.*
17. NAC. RG 150, Accession 1992-3/166, file 760-48.
18. Quoted in J.M. Bruce, *Aeroplanes of the Royal Flying Corps* (London: Putnam, 1982), p. 454.
19. Brereton Greenhous (ed.), *A Rattle of Pebbles: The First World War Diaries of Two Canadian Airmen* (Ottawa: Dept. of National Defence, Directorate of History, 1987), p. 79.
20. Arthur Bishop, *Courage of the Early Morning*, p. 31.

21. Ibid., p. 36.

22. To Margaret Burden, 14 July 1916.

23. Arthur Bishop, *Courage of the Early Morning*, p. 38.

24. To Margaret Burden, 14 July 1916.

25. NAC, RG 150, Accession 1992-3/166, file 760-48.

26. *The Times*, 26 Jan 1931, p. 12, St. Helier obituary.

27. C.S. Forester, in his introduction to W.S. Chalmers, *Life and Letters of David, Earl Beatty* (London: Hodder & Stoughton, 1951), p. xxiv.

28. Arthur Bishop, *Courage of the Early Morning*, pp. 40–41.

29. *Winged Warfare*, p. 30.

30. Bruce, *Aeroplanes of the Royal Flying Corps*, p. 242.

31. H.G. Anderson, *The Medical and Surgical Aspects of Aviation* (London: H. Frowde, 1919), p. 43.

32. *Winged Warfare*, p. 30.

33. Ibid., p. 33.

34. Ibid., pp. 33–35.

35. Ibid., p. 37.

36. Mathieson, p. 19.

37. To Margaret Burden, 22 Jan and 28 Feb 1917.

38. Ibid., 4 March 1917. Ball had, in reality, two DSOs, one MC and a *Croix de Guerre*!

39. Ibid., 28 Feb 1917.

Chapter 2: A Pilot at the Front

1. A.G. Lee, *No Parachute: A Fighter Pilot in World War I* (London: Jarrolds, 1968), p. 122.

2. W.M. Fry, *Air Of Battle* (London: Kimber, 1974), p. 136.

3. Merton College, *Register, 1900–1964* (Oxford: Clarendon Press, 1964).

4. *The Times*, 17 Jan 1922, Scott obituary.

5. I.G. Murray, The Honourable Society of the Inner Temple, to Anne Thomas, 24 Apr 1997, in author's possession.

6. British Army *List of Officers, 1909, 1910, 1911, 1912* and *1914*.

7. *The Times*, Scott obituary.

8. Ibid.

9. Lord Douglas of Kirtleside, *Years Of Combat* (London: Collins, 1963), p. 163.

10. *The Times*, Scott obituary.

11. Shores, Franks and Guest, *Above the Trenches*, p. 333.

12. Andrew Boyle, *Trenchard: Man Of Vision* (London: Collins, 1962), chaps. 1 and 3.

13. Fry, *Air of Battle*, p. 92.

14. Ibid., pp. 92–93.

15. H. Woodman, *Early Aircraft Armament: The Aeroplane and the Gun up to 1918* (London: Arms & Armour, 1989), p. 137.

16. A.J.L. Scott, *The History of 60 Squadron, RAF* (London: Heinemann, 1920), pp. 45–46.

17. W.A. Musciano, *Eagles of the Black Cross* (New York: Obolensky, 1965), pp. 55–56.

18. Boyle, *Trenchard*, pp. 198 and 206.

19. Jones, *War in the Air,*p. 334.

20. Ibid., pp. 334–335.

21. Sir Robert Thompson, *The Royal Flying Corps* (London: H. Hamilton, 1968), p. 106.

22. Letter to Margaret Burden, 12 March 1917.

23. See Brereton Greenhous, et al., *The Crucible of War, 1939-1945* [Canadian Official History] (Toronto: University of Toronto Press, 1994), pp. 168–9 and 195–6.

24. *Winged Warfare*, p. 44.

25. Ibid., p. 52.

26. Ibid., p. 55.

27. To Will Bishop, 29 March 1917.

28. To Margaret Burden, 29 March 1917.

29. See Mike Spick, *The Ace Factor: Air Combat and the Role of Situational Awareness* (Annapolis, Maryland: Naval Institute Press, 1988).

30. Jones, *War in the Air*, p. 406.

31. *Winged Warfare*, p. 106.

32. Spick, *The Ace Factor*, p. 77.

33. Combat Report, 6 April 1917, in DHH, 2001/9, Bishop Collection (Originals in PRO, Air 1/1225). Copies of all of Bishop's combat reports subsequently cited are to be found in this collection.

34. Musciano, *Eagles of the Black Cross*, p. 103.

35. Combat Report, 7 April 1917.

36. Peter Kilduff, *Richthofen: Beyond the Legend of the Red Baron*, (New York: John Wiley & Sons, 1993), p. 91.

37. Maurice Baring, *Flying Corps Headquarters, 1914–1918* Edinburgh: Blackwood, 1968, p. 213.

38. Scott, *History of 60 Squadron*, p. 40.

39. Fry, *Air of Battle*, pp. 137–138.

40. Douglas, *Years Of Combat*, p. 195.

41. Scott, *History of 60 Squadron*, p. 69.

42. Combat Report, 8 April 1917.

43. To Margaret Burden, 9 April 1917.

Chapter 3: Tricks of the Trade

1. S.F. Wise, *The Official History of the Royal Canadian Air Force*, Vol.1, *Canadian Airmen and the First World War* (Toronto: University of Toronto Press, 1980), p. 407.

2. Combat Report, 20 April 1917.

3. Franks, Guest and Bailey, *Bloody April … Black September*, p. 108.

4. Fry, *Air of Battle*, p. 95.

5. Combat Report, 20 April 1917.

6. Scott, *History of 60 Squadron*, p. 44n.

7. See Jones, *War in the Air*, p. 406.

8. Oliver Stewart, *Words and Music for a Mechanical Man* (London: Faber, 1967), p. 132.

9. Scott, *History of 60 Squadron*, p. 44.

10. Douglas, *Years of Combat*, p. 197.

11. *The Times*, 3 and 7 May 1917.

12. To Margaret Bishop, 21 April 1917.

13. Combat Report, 23 April 1917.

14. Second Combat Report, 23 April 1917.

15. Combat Report, 27 April 1917.

16. To Margaret Burden, 27 April 1917.

17. *Winged Warfare*, p. 134.

18. Combat Report, 25 April 1917.

19. *Winged Warfare*, p. 145.

20. Combat Report, 30 April 1917.

21. Scott's Combat Report, copy in author's possession.

22. To Margaret Burden, 30 April 1917.

23. *Winged Warfare*, pp. 145–46.

24. Kilduff, *Richthofen*, p. 102.

25. Combat Report, 30 April 1917.

26. Ibid., 2 May 1917.

27. To Margaret Burden, 1 June 1917.

28. *London Gazette*, 30135, 18 June 1917.

29. To Margaret Burden, 2 May 1917.

30. Combat Report, 2 May 1917.

31. Ibid.

32. Combat Report, 4 May 1917.

33. Fry, *Air of Battle*, p. 121.

34. Quoted in Markham to Norman Franks, 6 March 1995, Markham Papers (copy in author's possession).
35. Combat Report, 7 May 1917.
36. Ibid.
37. Musciano, *Eagles of the Black Cross*, p. 97.
38. Shores, Franks and Guest, *Above the Trenches*, pp. 59–60.
39. To Will Bishop, 14 May 1917.
40. See Shores, Franks and Guest, *Above the Trenches, passim.*
41. To Margaret Burden, 2 and 5 May 1917.
42. To Will Bishop, 14 May 1917.
43. Princess Marie Louise, *My Memories of Six Reigns* (London: Evans Bros., 1956), p. 185.
44. To Margaret Burden, 9 May 1917.
45. Ibid., 14 May 1917.
46. Combat Report, 26 May 1917.
47. Ibid., 27 May 1917.
48. Ibid., 1 June 1917.
49. Jones, *War in the Air*, p. 405.

Chapter 4: Flight of Fancy

1. To Margaret Burden , 18 April1917.
2. J. W.R. Taylor (ed), *Combat Aircraft of the World*, (New York: G.P. Putnam's Sons, 1969), pp. 115 and 117. See also the following Web page: http://www.theaerodrome.com/aircraft/france/nieuport/27.html
3 PRO, Air 1/708/10, "Principal Characteristics of Aeroplanes (French)."
4. Andrew Nahum, *The Rotary Aero Engine* (London: H.M.S.O., 1987), pp. 44–45.
5. Fry, *Air of Battle*, p. 135.
6. PRO, Air 1/1555/204/79/75, Acting CO 60 Sqn to 13th Wing

HQ, 30 June 1917.

7. PRO, Air 1/2239/209/42/6, III Brigade Daily Summary, 2 June 1917; *KoFl.2, Wochenbericht der Fliegerbande der 2 Armee, vom 31.5.17 bis 6.6.17* [translation], copy in DHH, W.A. Bishop Collection.

8. *Winged Warfare*, p. 186.

9. Ibid., p. 187.

10. DHH, W.A. Bishop Collection.

11. PRO, Air 1/1555/204/79/75, *loc.cit.*

12. DHH, SGR II, file 328. The provenance of this report (and two others, one for the previous week and the second for the same week by the neighbouring *KoFl.6*) is unclear, but they appear to have been acquired and translated by the late Fred Steiger, DHist's (as it then was) German expert, probably during and after one of his research trips to West Germany in the 1960s and early 1970s. Alternatively, they may have been donated by Phil Markham, who acquired them from his American friend, the late Ed Ferko, whose vast archive of German air material was deposited with the University of Texas.

13. *Winged Warfare*, p. 186–87.

14. David L. Bashow, *Knights of the Air: Canadian Fighter Pilots in the First World War* (Toronto: McArthur and Co., 2000), pp. 122–23.

15. DHH, SGR II, file 328.

16. Combat Report, 2 June 1917.

17. Arthur Bishop, *Courage of the Early Morning*, p. 99.

18. Taylor (ed), *Combat Aircraft of the World*, pp. 136–37.

19. Combat Report, 2 June 1917.

20. *Winged Warfare*, p. 190.

21. Ibid., pp. 190–91.

22. Ibid., p. 191.

23. Fry, *Air of Battle*, p. 135.

24. PRO Air 1/1555/204/79/75, loc.cit.

25. Eric Crundall, *Fighter Pilot on the Western Front* (London, 1975), p. 34.

26. Fry, *Air of Battle*, p. 136.

27. *Winged Warfare*, p. 192.

28. PRO, Air 1/1553//204/79/56.

29 A. A. Nicod, "Memories of 60 Squadron," in *Popular Flying*, Vol. 3, No 9, (December 1934).

30. Fry, *Air of Battle*, p. 136.

31. Quoted in Markham to N.R.L. Franks, 6 March 1995, Markham Papers (copy in author's possession).

32. Arthur Bishop, *Courage in the Air* (Toronto: McGraw-Hill Ryerson, 1992), p. 17.

33. PRO, Air 1/1554, 60 Sqn Record Book.

34. McCaffery, *Billy Bishop, Canadian Hero*, p. 211.

35. "Fabric," in *Cross & Cockade International*, Vol.16, No.4, (1985), p. 188.

36. Townsend to Markham, 7 Nov 1988, copy in author's possession.

37. Dan McCaffery, *Air Aces: The Life and Times of Twelve Canadian Fighter Pilots* (Toronto: Lorimer, 1990), p. 76.

38. DHH, SGR II, file 328.

39. PRO Air 1/1555/204/79/75, *loc. cit.*

Chapter 5: Flying High

1. Fry, *Air of Battle*, p. 136.

2. Ibid.

3. DHH, 2001/9, Bishop Collection.

4. Crook, *Evolution of the Victoria Cross*, p. 217.

5. Ibid., p. 263.

6. Markham, "The Early Morning Hours…" in *Over the Front*,

Vol. 10, No. 3 (Fall 1995), p. 242.

7. *Winged Warfare*, p. 209.

8. Combat Report, 8 June 1917.

9. Ibid.

10. *Winged Warfare*, p. 195.

11. Ibid., p. 213.

12. Combat Report, 15 June 1917.

13. Ibid., 24 June 1917.

14. DHH, Murray biog. file.

15. Quoted in F. Lowe, "Greatest of the Flying Madcaps," *Weekend Magazine*, Vol. 6, No. 46 (1956), p. 16.

16. Combat Report, 28 June 1917.

17. To Margaret Burden, 28 June 1917.

18. Ibid., 4 July 1917.

19. Wise, *Canadian Airmen*, p. 302.

20. Combat Report, 10 July 1917.

21. J. Warne, '60 Squadron: A Detailed History — Part 2,' in *Cross & Cockade (Great Britain) Journal*, No. 2 (1980), p. 60.

22. Ibid.

23. *Winged Warfare*, pp. 227–28.

24. DHH, 2001/9, Bishop Collection (III Brigade RFC, daily summary, 12 July 1917).

25. Combat Report, 13 July 1917.

26. DHH, 2001/9, Bishop Collection.

27. Ibid., (Squadron Record Book).

28. Bruce, *Aeroplanes of the Royal Flying Corps*, p. 475.

29. To Margaret Burden, 23 and 24 July 1917.

30. Combat Report, 28 July 1917.

31. To Margaret Bishop, 28 July 1917.

32. Bishop, *Courage of the Early Morning*, pp. 117–18.

33. *London Gazette*, 30466, 8 Jan 1917.

34. DHH, 2001/9, Bishop Collection ("Fights Return to August 11th, 1917").

35. *The Globe* (Toronto), 19 June 1917.

36. To Will Bishop, 4 Aug 1917.

37. To Louise Bishop, 8 Aug 1917.

38. To Margaret Burden, 7 Aug 1917.

39. Combat Report, 9 Aug 1917.

40. To Margaret Burden, 10 Aug 1917.

41. To Margaret Burden, 14 Aug 1917.

42. Ibid.

Chapter 6: A Statistical Interlude

1. Fry, *Air of Battle*, p. 178; Shores, Franks and Guest, *Above the Trenches*, p. 161.

Chapter 7: I Have Never Been So Furious in My Life

1. Arthur Bishop, *Courage of the Early Morning*, p. 124.

2. To Margaret Burden, 30 Aug 1917

3. Bruce, *Aeroplanes of the Royal Flying Corps*, p. 543.

4. Ibid., p. 536.

5. To Margaret Bishop, *née* Burden, 16 June 1917.

6. Ibid.

7. [J. McG. Grider], *War Birds: Diary of an Unknown Aviator* (New York: George H. Doran, 1926), p. 99.

8. Ibid., pp. 147–48.

9. Ibid., pp. 113–14.

10. Wise, *Canadian Airmen*, p. 485.

11. Taylor (ed), *Combat Aircraft of the World*, pp. 137 *passim*.

12. Cecil Lewis, *Sagittarius Rising* (Harrisburg, PA: Gininger, no date) pp. 126–27.

13. To Margaret Burden, 27 May 1917.

14. Combat Report, 27 May 1917.

15. Oberkommando des Heeres, *Der Weltkrieg 1914 bis 1918*, Bande XIV, Beilungen: Die Kriegsführung an der Westfront im Jahr 1918 (Berlin, 1944), Beilage 40.

16. These claims, and subsequent ones in this chapter, arte taken from Shores, Franks and Guest, *Above the Trenches*.

17. Combat Report, 28 May 1918.

18. To Margaret Bishop, 24 May 1918.

19. Combat Report, 30 May 1918.

20. Second Combat Report, 30 May 1918.

21. To Margaret Bishop, 30 May 1918.

22. To Margaret Bishop, 31 May 1918.

23. [Grider], *War Birds*, p. 162.

24. To Margaret Bishop, 26 May 1918.

25. [Grider], *War Birds*, p. 164.

26. Combat Report, 31 May 1918.

27. Second Combat Report, 31 May 1918.

28. To Margaret Bishop, 31 May 1918.

29. To Margaret Bishop, 2 June 1918.

30. [Grider], *War Birds*, p. 164.

31. Combat Report, 1 June 1918.

32. To Margaret Bishop, 6 June 1918.

33. Combat Report, 15 June 1918.

34. To Margaret Bishop, 16 June 1918.

35. [Grider], *War Birds*, p. 210.

36. Quoted in Wise, *Canadian Airmen*, p. 596.

37. Ibid., p. 597.

38. Ibid., p. 608.

39. Combat Report, 16 June 1918.

40. Combat Report, 17 June 1918.

41. Combat Report, 18 June 1918.

42. Elliot Springs, quoted in Robert E. Rogge, "War Birds Three," in *Cross & Cockade Journal*, Vol.6, No.2 (Summer 1965), p. 172.

43. Combat Report, 19 June 1918.

Epilogue

1. *National Post*, 14 August 1999, p. B5.

2. Ibid., 21 August 1999, p. B5.

3. See the following Web site: http://www.theaerodrome.com/forum/poll/results.shtml

4. See A.M.J. Hyatt, *General Sir Arthur Currie: A Military Biography* (Toronto: University of Toronto Press, 1987), pp. 10–12.

5. Wise, *Canadian Airmen*, p. 573.

6. McCaffery, *Billy Bishop, Canadian Hero*, p. 209.

7. Graves, "World War I's Flying Aces," *loc. cit.*

8. Shores, Franks and Guest, *Above the Trenches*, pp. 268–71.

9. Ibid., p. 255.

10. Paul Fussell, *Wartime: Understanding and Behaviour in the Second World War* (New York: Oxford University Press, 1989), preface.

Publisher's Afterword

From the very beginning of Dundurn Press, we have published quality books which explored and often celebrated Canada's military history. One of our earlier books was *King's Men, the soldier founders of Ontario* which studied in depth the contribution Butler's rangers and other loyalist soldiers made to the establishment of Ontario.

Through the years we have published books on all periods in Canada's military history and have been proud to co-publish with the Department of Nation Defence *Operation Friction*, the official history of the Canadian Forces in the Gulf War, as well as several books with the Canadian War Museum, books by such distinguished history as George Stanley (*Toil and Trouble*, the 1871 military expedition to the Red River) and Hereward Senior (*The Last Invasion of Canada* about the Fenians raids).

We also co-published with the Canadian War Museum an earlier book by Brereton Greenhous, *C-Force to Hong Kong* about the courageous but tragic defence of Hong Kong by Canadians in 1941. So when Ben approached us with a manuscript on Billy Bishop, Canada's most celebrated war hero, I was naturally enthusiastic.

This is a book that will disturb some people. While paying tribute to Bishop's unquestioned courage as a world war pilot, Greenhous argues that there is strong evidence to suggest that Bishop did not shoot down as many enemy aircraft as is generally thought nor is there any documented evidence that the early morning raid on a German airfield – which won Bishop the Victoria Cross – actually did take place. Greenhous further argues that Bishop's hero status was the creation of the British propaganda machine. Heroes were needed at this time in the war.

Some would argue that we shouldn't be publishing a book that attacks the reputation of a man who has been a Canadian military hero for eight decades, especially now when Canadian forces are involved in another war. But surely what our forces are doing now and have done so often in the past is to fight for our basic freedoms – and one important freedom is the right to seek the truth.

In presenting this book to the public, Dundurn remains committed to our original goal, publishing important contributions to the understanding of Canada's past.

Kirk Howard
March 2002

INDEX

Above the Trenches 193:
Adams, Lieut. W. Q.: 187
Aerial camera:
Aero-engines: characteristics, 108-9
  Beardmore, 41
  Renault, 46;
  Le Rhône J9a, 108, 120
  Le Rhône J9b, 108, prototype, 108, 109
Air of Battle: 95, 118
Air Ministry: 190
Air strategy: 61, 65,85, 86, 107, 176
Aircraft (general): 14
Aircraft (British/French):
  Avro 504, 37, 51
  BE 12a, 48; 135
  Bristol Fighter, 27, 175, 183, 191
  FE 2b, 48, 89;
  Maurice Farman *Série 11*, 46;
  Nieuport 17, easily broken, 62-3, 70, 75,
camera-equipped, 83, 87, 89, with prototype
engine 108;
    damage to B 1566, 123; last flight in B
1566, 141; other refs.; 135
  Nieuport 27, 108;
  RE 7, 38, 41;
  SE 5, 70, 71, 75, 100, 137, 141, 142
  SE 5a, 141, 172 , 173, 174, 175, 176, 177,
178, 182, 184, 194
  Sopwith Camel, 175, 176
  Sopwith Dolphin, 171-172, 173 174,
176, 177, 178
  Sopwith Pup, 51; 120-1
  Sopwith 1_ Strutter, 39, 59;
  Sopwith Triplane, 90;
  SPAD, 137, 174
Aircraft (German):
  Albatros C III, 103
  Albatros D I/II, 115 126, 135
  Albatros D III, 61, 62, 70, 73, 74, 87, 88,
90, 98, 99, 108, 114; differences with D I/II,
115; 123, 127, 134, 139, 141, 183, 187, 188,
191, 192
  Albatros D 5/D 5a, 176, 180, 181, 183
  Fokker *Dreidekker*-I, 177
  Fokker D-VII, 177, 187, 194, 196

  Gotha G IV, 85, 90;
  Halberstadt, 183
  LVG C-VI, 182, 183
  Pfalz D-III, 183, 184, 186, 188, 191, 194
  Zeppelin, 12, 47, 48, 85
Airfields:
  Anneux, 110, 111, 112, 115, 126, 127
  Awoignt, 113, 114, 115, 126
  Ayr, 172
  Bohain, 126
  Boistrancourt, 115, 124, 127
  Bray Dunes, 121
  Busigny, 112, 126
  Epinoy, 73
  Estes, 103, 113, 114
  Estourmel, see Boistrancourt;
  Filescamp, 55, 88, 100, 110, 114, 117,
126, 127, 144
  Guise, 114, 116, 126, 127, 139
  Gosport, 56f, 172
  Hendon, 47
  Houndslow, 173
  La Lovie, 183
  Middelburg, 114
  Netheravon, 37
  Petit Synthe, 178, 180, 183
  Proville, 125
  Roucourt,
  Ste. Olle, 111, 112, 114, 115, 126, 127
  St. Omer, 180, 187
  Turnberry: 189
  Upavon: 36, 171
Aitken, Sir Max: 16, 102, 133, 170
Albany, NY: 170
Alberich, Operation: 111
Aldis sight: 62, 174
Allenby, Gen. Sir Edmund: 60, 129
Almanach de Gotha: 101
Amiens, Battle of: 181
Anneux: see Airfields
Armentières: 135, 183, 191, 195
Argyll, Duke of: see Lorne, Marquis of.
Aribert, Prince of Anhalt-Dessau: 101f
Armies (British):
  First

Second, 185
Third, 60, 78
Armies (German):
2 Armee, 112, 114, 181
4 Armee, 114, 179, 181, 183, 185, 186, 187, 188, 191, 195
6 Armee, 180, 183, 186, 188, 191, 195
17 Armee, 181, 188
Arras: 55, 112, 115
Arras, Battle of: 78
Atkey, Capt. A. C.: 183
Awoignt: see Airfields
Ayr: see Airfields

Bailleul: 180, 183
Ball, Capt. Albert: meets B, 50;
fame in RFC, 76, 86
death, 99-100
credited with 44 victories, 100
plans raid on German airfield,
father's PR campaign for posthumous
VC, 102
other refs., 27, 74, 88, 143, 146, 185
Balloons, Kite: 14, 72-74
Banting, Sir Frederick: 199, 200
Bapaume: 112
Baring, Maurice: 74, 75; praises B,
Barker, Major William G.: VC citation, 205
Bashow, David L.: 24, 113
Beaverbrook, Lord: see Aitken, Sir Max
Belaney, Archie: 200
Bell-Irving, Capt, Alan: 75, 76
Benbow, Capt. Edwin (Lobo): 183-4, 186
Biache St.Vaast: 82
Billy Bishop: Canadian Hero: 22, 124, 205
Billy Bishop Goes To War: 17,
Billy Bishop, VC: 23
Birkenhead, Earl of: see Smith, F.E.
Bishop, Kilbourne: 29
Bishop, Louisa: 29
Bishop, Margaret: 29, 169
Bishop, Margaret, née Burden::
Bishop, Will: 29, 30, 45
Bishop, William Arthur: 16, 42, 45, 115, 124, 144
Bishop, Lieut-Col. William Avery (Billy): ninth in popular ranking of Cdn heroes, 13; courage, 13, 23; observer, 13; author, 15; death, 17; victory claims, 20-21; birth, 29; appearance, 29; youthful psychology, 29, 30; hobbies, 29; schooling, 30; at RMC, 31; cheating at RMC and rusticated, 31; class standings, 31; unmilitary, 32; cadet promotions, 33; graduating year, 32; commissioned in Missisauga Horse, 33; 7th CMR, 34; to England, 34; pleurisy, 36; joins

21 Sqn, 37; trains as observer, 37; first flight, 37; first crash, 38; 1914-1915 Star, 40; wounded, 42; knee injury, 42; vehicle accident, 42; concussion, 42; infected tooth, 42; nerves, 42, 81; alleges strained heart, 43; varicose veins, 43; meets St. Helier, 43; leave to Canada, 45; engaged to Margaret Burden, 45; to England, 46; pilot training, 46-7; night flying, 49; meagre flying skills, 49; first imaginary combat, 49-50; claims recommended for command of flight, 50; meets Ball, 50; to CFS, 50; forced landings, 51; fatalism, 51; joins B Flight, 55; first flight over enemy lines, 66; formation flying, 66-7; first witnessed victory, 67-8; abilities, 69; joins C Flight, 69; acting flight cdr, 69; disastrous patrol, 70; second witnessed victory, 70; first solo sortie, 70; 'balloon busting', 72-4, 88; awarded MC, 74; his charm, 77-8; saves Scott, 78; five sorties in one day, 87; promoted captain, 89; gfictitious fight with Von R, 90–2; posibly recommended for VC, awarded DSO, 93, 94; exhausted, 94, 101; shares credit with Fry, 95-6; leading Imperial ace, 100; 2 June 17 (VC raid), 107-128; recommended for VC, 129; 'good job' waiting in CFC, 133; paucity of claims in Scott's absence, 136; shaky nerves, 137; third witnessed victory, 140; fictitious crash, 144-5; recommended for second DSO, 145; media hint at VC, 147; awarded VC, 149; Imperial 'ace of aces', 149; to England, 150; statistical record with 60 Sqn., 151-167; VC, DSO, MC investiture, 169; Bar to DSO, 169; promoted major, 170; to Canada, 170; marriage, 170; to British War Mission, 170; writes Winged Warfare 170; to England, 171; command of 85 Sqn, 171; equipped with SE 5a, 174; to France, 178; resumes air fighting, 178; to be recalled to England, 188; supports idea of CFC, 190; posted to Home Establishment, 191; to be promoted lieut-col, 191; neglect of Springs and Grider, 193; last day of fighting, 194; statistical record with 85 Sqn, 196-7; fourth witnessed victory, 198; awarded DFC, 198; no Bar to VC, 198; his courage, 201; summary of service with 60 Sqn, 202-4; with 85 Sqn, 204; credited with 72 victories, 205; real total, 204; citations for gallantry decorations, 207-9
Bishop, Worth: 29, 34
'bloody April': 51, 63, 81, 91
Boelcke, Hauptmann Oswald: 64, 75
Boer War: 12
Bohain:see Airfields
Bois du Biez: 183
Boistrancourt: see Airfields

FlA (A) 269, 124
  Other refs., 63, 116, 126, 135
Flying skills: 46-7
Flying stress: 41
Folkestone, England: 34, 36
Formation flying: 66
Forster, W.E.: 44
Foster mounting: 61, 82, 141
France: 34, 36, 40, 85, 173
Fry, Lieut. William M.: assessment of Scott, 56;
  flying accident, 63; assessment of B, 77;
differs from B on air combat, 95-8; experience,
97; declines to accompany B on VC raid, 109;
account of B's return from VC raid, 118-120;
damage to B's machine after VC raid, 122;
awarded MC, 130; other refs. , 61, 133, 135
Flying, a dangerous occupation: 13
Fussell, Paul: 206

Gass. Lieut. C. G.: 183
George, Lloyd, prime minister of Britain: 44
George V, King: 44, 85, 101, 132, 169, 173
German air service: 14
Germany: 32
Geroj SSSR Medalj Zolotaja Zvezda: 11-12
Gosport, Hants.:see Airfields
Graves, Major Evelyn: 55, 56, 59
Graves, Timothy: 24, 205
Gray, Charlotte: 199, 200
Gray, John: 17
Great War: see First World War.
Grey County, Ontario: 29
Grey Owl: see Belaney, Archie
Grider, Lieut. John (Mac): 172, 173, 174,
184, 185, 186, 187, 188, 193, 194
Guelph: 16
Guemappe: 88
Guise:
Gunner ?: 142, 145
Gurdon, Capt. J. E.: 195
Guynemer, Georges: 86, 143

Haig, Gen. Sir Douglas: 130
*Hanging A legend: The NFB's Shameful
Attempt to Discredit Billy Bishop, VC*: 19
Hannover, Germany: 57
Hawker, Major Lanoe: 27, 75
Hayne, Capt. E. T.: 191
Helena, Princess: 44
Henderson, Sir David: 59
Hendon:see Airfields
Henin-Liètard: 136
Higgins, Col. J.F.A.: 60, 93, 129, 130, 139
History of 60 Squadron: 84
Home Defence: 48, 49

Home Establishment: 135, 136
Hooglede: 192
Horne, Lieut. Spencer: 78, 124, 133, 140,
147, 148, 172, 178, 182, 184, 186
Houlthem: 188
Houlthulst Forest: 179
Houndslow: see Airfields
House of Commons: 44
Howe, Lieut. F. C.: 188
Hozier, Clementine: see Churchill,
Clementine.
Hughes, Sir Sam: 33, 34, 133
Hypoxia: see Oxygen.

Inner Temple: 57
Internet poll: 200
Italy: 116
Izel-le-Hameau: seer Airfields, Filescamp
Izel-les-Esquerchin: 103

Jagdgeswader 1: 175, 176
Jagdstaffeln (Jastas): 63, 64, 114, 134
    Jasta Boelcke, 125
    Jasta 4, 175
    Jasta 5, 115
    Jasta 6, 175
    Jasta 10, 82, 175
    Jasta 11, 64, 91, 92, 99, *175*
    Jasta 12, 112
    Jasta 20, 113, 114
    Jasta 26, 114
Jenkins, Capt. W.S.: 180
Jones, Capt. Ira: 21f, 183

Kelly, 2nd Lieut. E.T.S.: 180
Kemmel: 180
Kemp,Sir Edward: 133, 189
Kennedy-Cochran-Patrick, Major W.J.C.: 138,
139, 144
Ketten: 64
Kid Who Couldn't Miss, The: 18
King, prime minister Mackenzie: 199
Kingston, Ontario: *170*
Kite Balloons: 72-4, 88, *186*
Knight, Capt. Arthur: 76
*Knights of the Air: Canadian Fighter Pilots in
the First World War*: 24, 113
Kommandeur der Flieger (KoFl.2): 112, 114,
123
Kommandeur der Flieger (KoFl.6): 114
Köppe, *Leutnant*: 124

La Gorgue: 187
Langan-Byrne, Lieut. Patrick: 75
Lark Hill: 38

Laurier, Sir Wilfrid: 45
Laventie: 192
Le Cateau:115
Le Cateau, Air Battle of: 176
League of World War I Aviation Historians: 25
Leakey, Sgt. N.G., KAR: 12
Lee, Arthur: 55
Lens: 92, 136
Leonard, Lieut-Col Ibbotson: 34, 37, 39
Leonard, Sarah: 40
Lewis, Capt. Cecil: 177
Lewis machine-gun: 38, 61-2, 119, 141, 174, 176
Liberal Party of Canada: 29, 30
Lille: 134, 135
Little, Flight Cdr. Robert A.: 100, 140
Lloyd, Lieut. ?: 135
'Lobo': see Benbow, Capt. Edwin
London , England: 48, 50, 56, 85, 133
London Gazette: 86, 93
London, Ontario: 34
Lorne, Marquis of: 101
Luke, Capt. T. C.: 188

Macedonia: 116
MacLaren, Capt. Donald: 22
Macready, Lieut.-Gen. Sir C. F. N.: 131, 132
Mannock, Major Edward: 21f, 100, 178, 183, 188, 189, 191, 193, 205
Maria Theresa, Order of: 12
Marie Louise, Princess: 44, 101, 102, 132, 169, 173, 201
Markham, Philip: 19, 24, 25, 96, 122, 132
Martin-Leake, Lieut A.: 171f
Mary Louise, Princess: 101
Mary, Queen: 101, 102
Mathiesen, William D.: 23, 49
McCaffrey, Dan: 22, 24, 124, 144, 205
McCudden, Capt. James: 100, 171, 178, 181, 185, 188, 205
McGregor, Lieut. ?: 178, 186
McKenzie, J.R.: 30
Medal of Honor, U.S.: 11, 12
Mention in Despatches (MiD):
Merton College: 57
Mesopotamia: 116
Messines, Battle of: 135, 136
Messenger, Charles: 24
Middelburg: see Airfields
Military Cross: 41
Ministry of Defence: 132
Mississauga Horse: 33
Molesworth, Lieut. W.E.: 79, 146, 147, 148
Monchy-le-Preux: 92, 144
Montreal: 170

Morale: 176
Morrison, Major Gen. E. W. B., 190
Murray, Lieut. Gladstone: 135, 136

Nachrichterblatt der Luftstreitkräfte: 128
National Archives of Canada (NAC): 40
National Defence, Dept. of (DND):
Directorate of History, (DHist), now
Directorate of History and Heritage, (DHH),
24; other refs. 17, 20, 144
National Film Board (NFB): 18, 19
National Post: 13, 14
Netheravon: see Airfields
Neuve Eglise: 180, 195
Neuville-St. Remy: 111
Neuville-Vitasse: 111
Newfoundland: 18
Newlands, Airman 1st Class: 180
New York, New York: 17
New Zealand: 57
Nicod, Sgt. A. A.: 122
Night flying: 47-8
Nottingham:
Nungesser, Charles: 86

Ontario: premier of, 16; rural standards of, 29
Oostkamp: 114
Ottawa, Ontario: 17, 170
Over The Front: 25
Overseas Ministry of Canada: 133
Owen Sound, Ontario: 29, 50, 170
Oxford University: 44
Oxygen, lack of: 89

Palm Beach, Florida:
Parachutes: 14
Passchendaele: 179, 180
Pearson, Lester B.: 14
Perley, Sir George: 137, 189
Permanent Force:
Peterson, Eric: 17
Petit Synthe: see Airfields
Ploegsteert: 194, 195
'Poetic licence': 17, 144
Portland Square: 101, 102
Pour Le Mérite: 11
Pretyman, Lieut-Col. George F.: 60, 93, 121, 129, 139,
Prince of Wales: 85
Propaganda: 21, 26, 27, 85, 102-3, 149, 170,
Proville: see Airfields
Public Works, Department of: 31

Quéant-Drocourt line: 92

Rees, Major Lionel: 27, 75
Ritterkreuz: 11
Roberts, Carl: 58
Robinson, Capt. W. Leefe: 12, 27, 47, 48
Rosebery, Earl of:
Ross, Capt. C.G.: 180
Roucourt: 91
Roulers: 182
Royal Air Force (RAF): 14, 22, 99, 176, 190
Royal Canadian Air Force (RCAF): 14, 16
Royal Family, The: 27
Royal Flying Corps (RFC):
    Communiqués, 99, 123, 137, 185
    Headquarters, Weekly Machine-Gun
return, 119
    III Brigade, 60, 140
    12th (Corps) Wing), 60
    13th (Army) Wing, 60
    strength, 65; losses, 65-6, 81, 85; danger of
morale breakdown, 76, 84-5, 93, 131, 132, 201
    other refs., 13 *passim*
RFC hospital, Bryanston Square:
Royal Military College of Canada (RMC):
standards, 30; Regulations, 31; yearbook, 31-2;
other refs, 34, 46, 201
Royal Naval Air Service (RNAS): 27, 90, 99,
138, 176, 178
Rumbeke: 182
Rupprecht, *Kronprinz* of Bavaria: 175
Russia: 116
Rutherford, Lieut. W.J.: 135
Rutledge, ?: 38

'Sad Case of Billy Bishop, VC, The': 19
Sailly-sur-le-Lys: 192
Salisbury, Lord: 37
Salisbury Plain: 37, 46
Salmond, Sir John: 176, 188
Sarnia, Ontario: 22
Scaramanga, 2nd Lieut. J. j>: 195
Schafer, Lieut. K.: 87
School of Military Aeronautics:
School of Special Flying, Gosport: 56f, 172
Scott, Major A. J. L. (Jack): birth, 57;
    schooling in Germany, 57; Merton
College,
    Oxford, 57; Master of Draghounds, 57
    obituary, 57; joins RFC, 58; crippled in
crash, 58; injured again in post-war crash, 58f;
flight cdr in 43 Sqn, 59; command of 60 Sqn.,
59; bond with Trenchard, 59-60; encourage-
ment of B, 76; ambitious for others, 76; wound-
ed, 138; to ommand 11th (Army) Wing, 138;
other refs, 23 *passim*
Scott, Henry Alan: 57

Second World War: 16, 18
Secord, Laura: 200
Senate of Canada: 18, 19
Sidebottom, Lieut. William: 191
Smith, Lieut. D. E.: 191
Smith, F.E.: 44-5, 57, 59, 60, 102, 132
Smith, Capt. F. R.: 187
Smith-Barry, Major Robert: 56f
South Africa: 60
South African War: see Boer War
South-East circuit: 57
South London sessions: 57
Southend: 48
Spandau machine-gun: 62
Springs, Lieut. Elliot: 181, 184, 186, 193
Squadron Record Book: 124
Squadrons:
    No.1, 180
    No. 2 (AFC), 187
    No. 7, 135
    No. 8 RNAS ('Naval Eight'), 140
    No. 11, 47, 97, 99
    No. 12, 97
    No. 20, 180
    No. 21, 37, 40, 41
    No. 22, 183, 195
    No. 37, 48, 49,
    No. 40, 184
    No. 43, 59;
    No. 48, 27
    No. 54,
    No. 56, 74, 99
    No. 60, 22 *passim*
    No. 74, 183, 188, 189
    No. 85, 25, 171, 172, 173, 178, 180,
189, 198
    No. 203, 191
    No. 209, 188
    No. 210, 180
Staden: 192
Star, 1914-1915: 40-1
Statistical tables: B with 60 Sqn: 151-164,
with 85 Sqn, 196-7
Steenwerk: 180
Stewart-Mackenzie of Seaforth, Susan Mary:
see St. Helier
St. Cyr, Lili: see Van Schaak
St. George, Order of:
St. Helier, Lady (Granny): 12, 43-5, 50, 56,
60, 101, 132, 146, 169, 171, 201, 205
St. Omer: 130, 180, 182
Ste. Olle: see Airfields
Sussex Yeomanry: 57
Sutton's Farm: 48, 49, 50

Taylor, Stewart: 24, 113
Thayer, Lieut. A.T.: 180
Thayre, Capt. F.J.H.: 100
Times, The: 26, 57, 85, 102
Toronto Globe: 146
Toronto, Ontario: 33, 170
Townsend, Lieut. Philip: 124
Trenchard, Major-Gen Sir Hugh: 41, 59, 61, 65, 74, 75, 86, 130, 138, 139, 149, 176
Trigg, F/O L A., RNZAF: 12
Turnberry: see Airfields
Turner, Lieut. Gen. Sir Richard: 137, 170, 189

U-boat: 12
United States Army Air Service: 172
United States of America: 18, 170,
Unknown Soldier (UK): 13
Unknown Warrior (US): 13
Upavon: see Airfields
Upham, Capt. Charles: 171f

Van Schaak, Marie: 200
Vancouver Island: 18
Vancouver East Cultural Centre: 17
Vert Galand: 88
'Vic' formation: 67
Vickers machine-gun: 119, 141, 174
Victoria Cross (VC): review committee, 121, 130; Royal Warrant, 11, 12, 131; destruction of files, 132-3; other refs, 11 *passim*
Victoria, Queen: 101
Victory Claims: 22
Victory Medal: 40
Vienna, Peace of: 44

Vimy Ridge: 61, 78
Vis-en-Artois: 83, 88
Vitry-en-Artois: 72, 82, 87, 88, 148
Von Richthofen, *Freiherr* Manfred: 23, 26, 64, 74, 75, 76, 85, 90, 91, 92, 93, 99, 143, 175, 176
Von Richthofen, *Leutnant* Lothar: 91, 92, 99
Voss, *Leutnant* Werner: 98, 99, 176

Wancourt: 92
Warbirds: Diary of an Unknown Aviator: 173
War Amputations of Canada: 19
War Office (UK):
    destruction of files, 26; committee for VC review, 121, 130; other refs., 36, 37, 38, 44, 59
Weather: 35-6
Weekly Activity Reports: see *Wochenberichten*
Western Front: 36, 178, 190, 201
Whitehall: 27, 56
Wigham, Major-Gen. Sir Robert: 131
Wilhelm II, *Kaiser*: 91
Windsor Castle: 102, 132
Winged Warfare: treated as primary source, 15 *passim*
Winston Churchill: 58
Wochenberichten (Weekly Activity Reports): 112, 114, 123
Wolff, Lieut. Kurt: 87
World War II Investigator: 24

Young, Lieut. ?: 140
Ypres: 180, 182

Zeppelin: see Aircraft
Zillebeke Lake: 188, 191